"Hester has given us three major concepts—narrative, belonging, and diversity—that could deeply enrich theological education. He has given us examples from his experience as a pastor, professor of pastoral theology, and counselor. I see how these concepts can enrich the teaching of my own discipline, the history of Christianity. And I also see how they can enrich the teaching of other disciplines. This is, in fact, theological education in a new key."

—G. THOMAS HALBROOKS,
retired president, Colgate Rochester Crozer Divinity School

"Reader, beware. Richard Hester's *Theological Education in a New Key* invites you on a harrowing journey. Both memoir and challenge to the traditional theological education, Hester uses his own story and reflections on his ministerial career as pastor and professor to courageously confront his blind spots and shortcomings around race and the meaning of Other. With a confessional tone, Hester allows you to accompany him into his own learning that is subversive— and sacred."

—LOGAN C. JONES,
ACPE certified educator, retired

"Hester's account of rewriting this book when confronted with the stunning realization of his Whiteness is akin to Augustine's *Confessions*, and his integrity offers a brave witness that will captivate and challenge every reader. Those tired of hearing theological education in discordant tones looking for a melody worthy of our current moment would do well to steep themselves in Hester's vision."

—W. BENJAMIN BOSWELL,
creator, Confronting Whiteness

"At the heart of progressive teaching are teacher and student learning alongside one another. As a career publisher of books incorporating progressive pedagogies, I recognize models for putting such approaches into practice when I encounter them. Hester's book is this kind of roadmap. With uncommon humility and courage, he unpacks his own story as a teaching text and shows how centering humanity—both the teacher's and students'—provides a pathway to new understanding."

—VICKI BOYD,
former executive vice president, Houghton Mifflin Harcourt

"Richard Hester has distilled his decades of theological teaching into an understanding that upends our conventional thinking. He shifts the focus of transformative learning from the teacher to what he calls the inner 'textbooks' of his students. Teaching from his own inner 'textbook,' Hester, awakening to his own embedded Whiteness, rewrote the manuscript with this awareness in mind. This book will awaken your curiosity about another way to see education by recovering its Latin origin, 'to bring forth.'"

—MAHAN SILER,
retired pastor, Pullen Memorial Baptist Church

"Dick Hester was my professor and mentor in seminary. The problem-based, relational education that defined his teaching initiated the practices I now follow as a university educator. These practices are critical to my world of leadership education and are desperately needed in our world today."

—JANICE E. ODOM,
director, The Caldwell Fellows, North Carolina State University

"Richard Hester steers teachers from a professor-dominant posture toward fostering interactive peer-driven encounters. Regardless of one's profession, reading this book can shape that profession into a vocation that influences others and, in turn, learns from them. I wish I had read this fifty years ago!"

—C. MICHAEL HAWN,
university distinguished professor emeritus of church music,
Perkins School of Theology, Southern Methodist University

Theological Education in a New Key

Theological Education in a New Key
Narrative, Belonging, Diversity

RICHARD L. HESTER
foreword by Tom W. Boyd

CASCADE *Books* · Eugene, Oregon

THEOLOGICAL EDUCATION IN A NEW KEY
Narrative, Belonging, Diversity

Copyright © 2025 Richard L. Hester. All rights reserved. Except for brief quotations in critical publications or reviews, no part of this book may be reproduced in any manner without prior written permission from the publisher. Write: Permissions, Wipf and Stock Publishers, 199 W. 8th Ave., Suite 3, Eugene, OR 97401.

Cascade Books
An Imprint of Wipf and Stock Publishers
199 W. 8th Ave., Suite 3
Eugene, OR 97401

www.wipfandstock.com

PAPERBACK ISBN: 979-8-3852-2363-3
HARDCOVER ISBN: 979-8-3852-2364-0
EBOOK ISBN: 979-8-3852-2365-7

Cataloguing-in-Publication data:

Names: Hester, Richard L., author. | Boyd, Tom W., foreword.

Title: Theological education in a new key: narrative, belonging, diversity / Richard L. Hester; foreword by Tom W. Boyd.

Description: Eugene, OR: Cascade Books, 2025 | Includes bibliographical references.

Identifiers: ISBN 979-8-3852-2363-3 (paperback) | ISBN 979-8-3852-2364-0 (hardcover) | ISBN 979-8-3852-2365-7 (ebook)

Subjects: LCSH: Pastoral theology. | Storytelling—Religious aspects—Christianity. | Education—Religious aspects—Christianity.

Classification: BV4011.3 H49 2025 (paperback) | BV4011.3 (ebook)

VERSION NUMBER 07/30/25

Unless otherwise stated all biblical quotations are from the New Revised Standard Version Bible, copyright 1989, Division of Christian Education of the National Council of Churches in the United States of America

For my grandchildren, my hope for the future

Kate Fialko
Andy Fialko
Nathan Hester
Rachel Hester

Contents

Foreword by Tom W. Boyd | ix

Acknowledgments | xiii

1. When You Can't Put It into Words | 1
2. Called to Be a Pastor in a Time of Racial Conflict | 19
3. Early Childhood Memories and Jesus' Parables | 37
4. Opening Students' Inner Textbooks with Problem-Posing Education | 60
5. Families: Where Theology Begins | 80
6. The Power of Belonging: Education with Peer-Led Student Groups | 107
7. Narrative Means to Educational Ends | 123
8. Know Your Story and Lead with It: The Sustaining Pastoral Excellence Project | 149
9. Conclusion by an Unfinished Teacher | 171

Bibliography | 173

Foreword

> I believe most people understand abstract ideas more clearly if they hear them through stories, and so I try to convey difficult and abstract ideas through the medium of my own life
>
> —Douglas Hofstadter

Reading this book captured my imagination on three accounts. First, it takes the subject of personal narrative to a depth I had not conceived, making it a primary aspect of education. Furthermore, the book reveals how its narrative approach *for both student and teacher* brings the humanity of participants to the center of the educational experience.

In the second place, this book introduced me to a concept of how the personal narrative actually functions for both students and teachers. This is revealed when Hester describes students' personal narratives as *the student's inner textbook*. This came to me as a revelation of a long neglected resource for learning.

Finally, the idea that narrative education is subversive activity proved compelling. I have long believed that challenging the sociocultural status quo belongs to the mission of higher education. Hester puts the case well, when he says "that life-changing learning lures students out of the trance of conventional wisdom." Hester ties this phrase to his idea of the student's inner textbook, when he writes, "The soul is accessible only through narrative."

Foreword

Reflecting on the three themes running through this book took me back to my own vocation as an educator. Over a teaching career of forty-three years I struggled repeatedly with issues related to pedagogy. Like the book's author, I was never given guidance in the methods of teaching. The only helpful suggestion I ever received came from a seasoned colleague: "You teach best when you stop teaching and become a fellow learner with your students." Sage advice, I found, and liberating. This book reveals how its author came to a similar understanding through his transformation into a narrative educator. He confesses as much when he says, "I gradually let go of my role as teacher and invited members to pick up the teaching roles. The seminar became an egalitarian learning laboratory."

When I began my teaching career as a professor of philosophy, I entered the sacred precinct of the classroom with a head full of the problems, propositions, and processes the discipline had provided me. What I soon learned, rather like Hester, was that I only offered students *banking education* as he calls it. My teaching was all objective and utterly abstract, as philosophy can singularly be. The blank and bewildered stares of students soon informed me that my teaching had to change.

I discovered that narrative is by far the best way to actually *engage* students and draw them immediately into the circle of learners. I did not know, however, the depth and primacy of narrative necessary to capture what Hester calls *the soul of education*. By this phrase, he refers to the core of what allows learning to take place. I had by no means arrived at this core.

For years I simply included stories from literature, from intellectual writings, and from my own imagination. These helped, but they failed to go deep enough. Eventually I learned to tell more *personal* stories out of my own life. This proved somewhat more compelling to students and seemed to draw a closer bond between my students and me. The most serious issue I had to face was that the best stories are not ones that made me the *hero*. In this book the stories that Hester tells about himself reveal his failures as well as his successes.

Foreword

My personal stories allowed students to become even more engaged, but still, I was not and never did become adequately aware of narrative at the depth described in this book. That is, I did not recognize that the most personal narratives of students themselves, their inner textbooks, could be a transformative resource for drawing them fully into their own education.

I taught large classes of up to two hundred students. How could I teach these large classes in such a personal way? Hester answers this question with his case for small class subgroups that meet regularly to work on the connection between their personal stories and the subject matter of the course. These subgroups are led by advanced students. These advanced students meet regularly as a group with the teacher to consider what is going on in the groups and to further their understanding of group facilitation.

The closest I ever came to opening the inner textbook of students was an assignment I gave to students on their second day in a summer school course on existentialism. I asked them to write a paragraph on what they were thinking as they entered the classroom that morning. I learned three things. First, I learned that they were not at all thinking about the course they were beginning. Second, I learned that no two of them were occupied with the same interests. Third, I learned that some of them brought into the room formidable personal crises. For instance, one student had been told by her husband that morning that if she came to the class their marriage would be over. Rather than study existentialism by reading about old dead men from afar, she entered the class with her own existential crisis. She had become what the course was about.

Hester elicits stories like this from his students but then asks them to use that story, along with other personal narratives, as a text for the course—along with the required printed texts. Paying attention to the inner text challenges teachers to make students' experience a resource as important as the subject matter of the course. And this approach calls forth the teacher's own narrative.

Most of us academic types are inclined to place the subject matter of the course, as significant and worth learning as it may be, as the singular interest in the class. Students become secondary. As I once heard a faculty colleague complain, "I could be a much better teacher if only I had better students." On the contrary, students are taken seriously, as this book insists, allowing the subject matter to radiate with *pertinence*, and pertinence inspires learning more than any other factor.

One thing more. This use of student narrative as a central pedagogical resource opens students to critical insight into their own cultural world. As they probe more deeply into their own stories, they begin to sense how culture has shaped, as well as limited, them. When people find their own inner locus and its integrity, they stand both within and over against their culture and its restraints.

If you are interested in how people learn and how learning can have a lasting, even life-long effect, I invite you to explore the wisdom of this book for yourself.

Tom W. Boyd, David Ross Boyd Professor Emeritus of Philosophy and Religious Studies, University of Oklahoma

Tom Boyd died on February 13, 2024, before he could see the publication of this book. He wrote this foreword in response to an earlier draft of the book; however, his main stream of thought nonetheless fits what I've written. His foreword continues here as part of his legacy. He taught philosophy at the University of Oklahoma for twenty-nine years and then taught in the Religious Studies Program for eleven additional years. He was awarded an honorary doctorate by the university in 2013.

Acknowledgments

THIS BOOK BEGAN IN my garage in 2016 when I pulled out a box that contained student term papers from classes I taught at Southeastern Baptist Theological Seminary in the late 1980s and early 1990s. I saved these papers because they were so personal and so compelling. The authors of the papers must remain anonymous, but they are the fertile soil and dynamic seeds that finally grew into this book. In one set of papers students told about their earliest childhood memories and related these to a parable of Jesus. In another set the papers described the formal and functional theology in the families in which the students grew up. I am deeply indebted to these students and grateful for their giving me permission to share their stories in this book.

Moving back in time, I must express my gratitude to the members of Parkview Baptist Church where I was pastor 1967–70 and where I got my first intimate lessons in racial relationships and how racial oppression was shaping the city of Gainesville, Florida. The book begins with that story.

Ulrike Guthrie edited the book through its several drafts before it ever went out as a proposal to a publishing house. Her work improved the manuscript immeasurably. She has been a friend and writing mentor. I am grateful to Tom Boyd, Robert Baird, and Mahan Silar for reading and critiquing early versions of the book.

On May 25, 2020, Minneapolis police officer Derek Chauvin murdered George Floyd. That event occurred about the same time I was participating in a workshop, "What Does It Mean to Be White?"

Acknowledgments

led by Benjamin Boswell, senior minister of Myers Park Baptist Church in Charlotte. These two events jolted me awake to face the fact that the manuscript I thought was finished, wasn't. It was utterly White, largely ignoring the racism that had infected this country since the first slaves were brought here in 1619. I was serving as Ben's organization development consultant, but now he was not only my client, he became my mentor in understanding my Whiteness. I had to rewrite the manuscript.

Once I discovered the Whiteness issue, I sought Black readers who could give me their view of the manuscript. They included Malu Fairley-Collins, clinical pastoral education coordinator for CaroMont Health in Gastonia, North Carolina, and vice president of the Alliance of Baptists; and Mia McClain, now pastor of Riverside Baptist Church in Washington, DC.

Members of the staff of Triangle Pastoral Counseling in Raleigh, North Carolina, contributed significantly to the chapter on "Narrative Means to Educational Ends."

Michael Hawn and Tom Halbrooks, both former colleagues of mine at Southeastern Baptist Theological Seminary, read and shared with me their wisdom about the most recent version of the manuscript.

I must give credit to two authors whom I have never met for their profound influence on this book. The first is William Herzog who wrote *Parables as Subversive Speech: Jesus as Pedagogue of the Oppressed*.[1] He found in the Brazilian educator Paulo Freire a way to understand and illuminate Jesus' use of parables. Freire wrote *Pedagogy of the Oppressed*[2] based on his literacy work of teaching peasants how to read and write. Freire and his teaching teams sought to teach reading and writing to peasants based on the peasants' own culture, idiom, and way of viewing the world, a worldview quite different than that of the privileged class. Herzog and Freire helped me understand

---

1. Herzog, *Parables as Subversive Speech*.
2. Freire, *Pedagogy of the Oppressed*. This thirtieth anniversary edition of this book has seen 750,000 copies sold worldwide.

Acknowledgments

how my students used Jesus' parables to unlock suppressed, often painful, and untapped stories of their lives.

Greg Lee, pastor of St. Paul and Wesley Chapel United Methodist Churches in Reidsville, North Carolina, in our twice a month conversations, from his perspective as a Black pastor, has helped me see things in my manuscript that in my Whiteness I was unable to see.

I am grateful for the support Greg Jarrell has offered me and for his recommendation that I seek to publish my book with Cascade.

1

When You Can't Put It into Words

In *Adventures of Huckleberry Finn*,[1] Mark Twain tells the story of the friendship that developed between Huck Finn and Jim, the runaway slave, as they floated on a raft down the Mississippi River. The grand narrative of slavery works on Huck's conscience telling him that it is wrong to hide and protect a runaway slave as Huck has done all along their journey.

At the heart of Huck's struggle is his knowledge that Jim cares for him and loves him—a love that has been demonstrated time and again on this long trip. He tried his best, he says, to find "places to harden me against him," but all that would come to mind was Jim's utter devotion to him.

However, the grand narrative of slavery does its work so relentlessly on his conscience that Huck decides he has to write a letter to Jim's owner, Miss Watson, to tell her where Jim is—an act that will return Jim to slavery. Huck believes that if he doesn't obey this grand narrative of slavery, he will go to hell. He writes the letter, but he keeps thinking of Jim's devotion to him. He recalls Jim's gratitude when Huck saved him from two men who were looking for runaway slaves.

> He was so grateful, and said I was the best friend old Jim ever had in the world, and the only one he's got now; and then I

1. Twain, *Adventures of Huckleberry Finn*.

happened to look around, and see that paper [the letter to Jim's owner]. It was a close place. I took it up and held it in my hand. I was a trembling because I'd got to decide, forever, betwixt two things, and I knowed it. I studied a minute, sort of holding my breath, and then says to myself: "All right, then, I'll go to hell"—and tore it up. It was awful thoughts, and awful words, but they was said. And I let them stay said; and never thought no more about reforming.[2]

The story of Huck and Jim borders on the *ineffable* as it carries in it the indescribable effect of White domination and the cruelty of slavery. In this narrative, through the words of his character Huck Finn, Mark Twain communicates how slavery does severe damage to the moral compass of White people and how Huck preserves his moral compass by doing the opposite of what the god of the culture tells him to do. Twain tells this story, and the entire story of Huck Finn, with such power that it prompted Ernest Hemingway to say, "All modern American literature comes from one book called *Huckleberry Finn*. There was nothing before. There has been nothing as good since."[3]

Huckleberry Finn does not *explain* what slavery does to human beings; the story takes us there. Its effect is ineffable. Which brings me to the title of this book, which is adapted from Susanne K. Langer's[4] *Philosophy in a New Key*,[5] which Harvard University Press published in 1942. In her book, Langer contended that the philosophical community wasn't paying attention to experience that is unspeakable, that cannot be expressed in discursive symbols—symbols that are

---

2. Hearn, *Annotated Huckleberry Finn*, 344.
3. Hearn, *Annotated Huckleberry Finn*, from the dust jacket.
4. Susanne K. Langer (1895–1985), with a PhD from Harvard, taught philosophy at Radcliffe, Wellesley, Smith, and other colleges while raising two sons and writing her first scholarly works. She was one of the first women in the United States to pursue an academic career in philosophy and among the first women to be considered a major American philosopher. She became a leading figure in the philosophy of art. She completed her career as chair of the philosophy department at Connecticut College. *Philosophy in a New Key* is her best known work and sold more than five hundred thousand copies in her lifetime. (This biographical information is from the Connecticut Women's Hall of Fame, of which Langer was a member.)
5. Langer, *Philosophy in a New Key*.

arranged in sentences, paragraphs, books. Discursive symbols are able to capture and express only a small percentage of human experience. The experience we cannot describe in discursive language has significant but neglected power. Langer's view of philosophy is my view of theological education—how, like Langer's critique of philosophy, theological education neglects what cannot be put into words—what can't be explained.

To make her case, Langer turns to music to say that "because the forms of human feeling are much more congruent with musical forms than with the forms of language, music can reveal the nature of feelings with a detail and truth that language cannot approach." Music expresses what is unspeakable in verbal language.[6] She names this unspeakable language *presentational symbolism* and the language we use to describe our experience in words *discursive symbolism* or language proper.[7] Philosophy in a new key is philosophy that recognizes and values presentational symbolism—the unspeakable—as different from our familiar rational, linguistic way of understanding the world.

In the presentational symbolism of music, says Langer, "the assignment of meanings is a shifting, kaleidoscopic play, probably below the threshold of consciousness, certainly outside the pale of discursive thinking." She writes that the lasting effect of music is "to make things conceivable rather than to store up propositions. Not communication but insight is the gift of music."[8]

Suzanne Langer's new key asks of theological education, "Are you paying attention to that aspect of human experience that is inexpressible in words but that nonetheless powerfully influences our thought, feelings, and volition?" To find the new key to theological education we must imagine that this key is invisible to us yet present and profoundly influential. Our discursive symbols—the words we ordinarily use—are inadequate for finding it or describing it.[9]

6. Langer, *Philosophy in a New Key*, 235.
7. Langer, *Philosophy in a New Key*, 97–99.
8. Langer, *Philosophy in a New Key*, 244.
9. A book that uses the same metaphor in its title as my metaphor of "new key" was

Theological Education in a New Key

USE OF THE WORD *KEY*

The title of this book is *Theological Education in a New Key*, and throughout the book I use the *key* metaphor. First, I follow Susanne Langer's use of the metaphor of a key to speak of what is *ineffable*, that which cannot be put into words. The morally corrupting power of slavery exceeds the words one may try to use to describe it. Huck Finn, however, points to this morally corrupting power in the narrative of his decision to go to hell to protect his friend Jim the runaway slave. I use three other words that, together with *ineffable*, describe my understanding of theological education in a new key—*narrative*, *belonging*, and *diversity*. At the end of each chapter I conclude with a synopsis of how these *keys* have appeared in the chapter.

CAPITALIZING *BLACK* AND *WHITE* FOR GRAMMATICAL JUSTICE AND EQUITY

This book capitalizes the words *Black* and *White* whenever they refer to race. This capitalization raises to awareness the fact that these racial designations refer to social constructions and not to an inherent condition of being Black or being White. John Palfrey and Kristen Mack, president and vice president of the MacArthur Foundation, make the case that in US history "many have attempted to systematically erase the ethnic identities of Black communities. Yet, Black culture has endured and flourished and continues to be a unique cultural identity today. We realize it is long past time to recognize it as such in the ways we write." Black is a positive indicator of personhood, culture, and history.[10] This fact stands out in the declaration, "Black lives matter!" And that is why I capitalize Black.

What about White and Whiteness? The MacArthur leadership states, "Choosing to not capitalize White while capitalizing other racial and ethnic identifiers would implicitly affirm Whiteness as

---

written by Robert McAfee Brown, *Theology in a New Key*. Brown's book explores Latin American liberation theology and its relevance for North American theology and practice. He doesn't use the "new key" metaphor as does Susanne Langer or as I do.

10. Palfrey and Mack, "Capitalizing Black and White," para 2.

the standard and norm. Keeping White lowercase ignores the way Whiteness functions in institutions and communities," and they cite this view from the Center for the Study of Social Policy: "The detachment of 'White' as a proper noun allows White people to sit out of conversations about race and removes accountability from White people's and White institutions' involvement in racism."[11] White and Whiteness are examples of *presentational symbolism*. To understand the invisible reality of Whiteness is to understand how racism is an issue within us as White persons. It sounds odd to say it, but we who are White don't know we're White. We do not grasp how being White entitles us to privileges and powers that are not available to people of color. We don't want to think of ourselves as holding a position of White supremacy over people who aren't White. Yet we do. It's bound up in the presentational symbolism that's mostly invisible to us.[12]

PURSUING PRESENTATIONAL SYMBOLISM

Stella called me on Thanksgiving Day to say she was at her wits end because she couldn't write the paper I'd assigned to my class. "I can draw it or paint it, but I'm not able to put words on paper." I told her to turn in whatever she could and I would consider it. She turned it in, and I accepted her well-done artistic response to the assignment. In doing this, I had to let go of what I understood to be my duty to evaluate a document written in discursive language.[13]

Stella became an art therapist, and I followed her career. For twenty-three years she served as the art therapist at a large federal prison hospital. Working from the perspective of *presentational symbolism*, she was able to transform spaces in the hospital with works of art. She supervised patients to paint a mural on the blank wall of a cancer treatment room where patients spent hours sitting and waiting for their chemotherapy to do its work. She supervised a group of

11. Palfrey and Mack, "Capitalizing Black and White," paras. 6–7.

12. The practice in this book of capitalizing the words Black and White when they refer to race does not apply to quoted material.

13. Stella later said of this event that it "changed my life" and was "a factor in making me an art therapist."

patients who created a giant artistic mobile that was lowered from the high ceiling of the atrium entrance to the prison hospital to music from the soundtrack of *2001: A Space Odyssey*, eliciting cheers from the patients and staff. She guided patients to create various artistic pieces that virtually transformed the prison hospital into an art gallery.

Because the hospital had no ritual to mark the death of patients, she developed one. She led a group of patients to make a quilt, and each square on the quilt represented a patient's life and death. She arranged for friends of the deceased to tell the quilt group about the one who had died, and the group took this testimony and created symbols to represent that person. Those symbols were then stitched into the quilt. "The quilt," said one of the patient inmates, "is our cemetery."

Stella understood the power of *presentational symbolism* and used it to bring beauty and inspiration to the prison patients, the staff, and visitors. The hospital became an artistic wonder, and it was created not by her but by the patient inmates themselves. As Stella worked every day with patients to bring artistic beauty to the halls and rooms and chapel of the prison hospital, she and the patients created *a narrative of redemption*. They redeemed a cold, sterile, prison environment by infusing it with artistic beauty.

MY DISCOVERY OF A NEW KEY TO THEOLOGICAL EDUCATION

I am writing this in 2022 in a time marked by a series of disruptive national events, of which three stand out: on May 25, 2020, the murder of George Floyd by a Minneapolis policeman; on January 6, 2021, an assault on the United States Capitol by an angry mob of Trump supporters; and on June 24, 2022, the Supreme Court decision in Dobbs v. Jackson that overturned the protection of the right to an abortion secured by Roe v. Wade. Each of these events comes out of the deep vein of racism in America, and each one is an expression of White supremacy.

Robert P. Jones in *White Too Long* writes that our society, our culture, makes it seem like there are inherent differences between Black and White persons, but that it isn't so. He calls for

> pulling back the veil on the fictional nature of whiteness.... For whiteness is the mortar holding together the fortress of white supremacy, and if it crumbles, those walls will inevitably collapse. Because of its binding importance, the idea of whiteness has been, and remains today, vigilantly defended. In fact, virtually nothing has proven too costly a sacrifice on the altar of its defense.[14]

His naming of these costly sacrifices includes the bloodbath of the Civil War, Jim Crow laws enforcing segregation, redlining barriers in real estate, and a criminal justice system that incarcerates millions of Black men and women—numbers far out of proportion to their share of the population. And this description does not include those who are put to death for crimes they may or may not have committed. Nor does it include the more than 4,500 African Americans who were lynched between 1877 and 1950.[15] "If one stops long enough to reflect on it," Jones writes, "the ransom this fiction has demanded to sustain itself is staggering."[16] The fiction of Whiteness and its presentational symbolism drives each of these three events.

THE MURDER OF GEORGE FLOYD

On May 25, 2020, Minneapolis police officer Derek Chauvin murdered George Floyd, a Black man, by holding him face down, handcuffed, with his knee on Floyd's neck as onlookers begged him to let Floyd up. He kept his knee on Floyd's neck until he died of asphyxiation after repeatedly pleading, "I can't breathe" and desperately asking for his mother. The entire tragic scene was recorded by eighteen-year-old Darnella Frazier on her cell phone and was soon viewed by a world-wide audience. Her video was advanced as evidence in

---

14. Jones, *White Too Long*, 19.
15. Jones, *White Too Long*, 13.
16. Jones, *White Too Long*, 19.

the trial and conviction of Derek Chauvin, and it helped to reignite the "Black Lives Matter" movement with new urgency. Ms. Frazier received a special citation from the Pulitzer Prize Board of Columbia University for her "transformative video that jolted viewers and spurred protests against police brutality around the world."[17]

Darnella Frazier's recording revealed the stunning cruelty of White domination perpetrated by a White policeman on a Black man until the policeman suffocated George Floyd to death. The "Black Lives Matter" movement declares that this White on Black cruelty by White police on Black victims occurs every day in this country. George Floyd's death isn't an exception. Black Americans account for roughly 14 percent of the US population but are killed by police at more than twice the rate of White Americans.[18] The invisible presentation symbolism of Whiteness drives each White on Black police overreach.

THE INSURRECTION AT THE UNITED STATES CAPITOL

On January 6, 2021, President Donald Trump held a rally of his supporters, some of them armed. Classified information from the Secret Service and FBI reported that protestors numbered 120,000 and that an estimated 1,200 entered the Capitol.[19] In that rally Donald Trump repeated his claim, a claim entirely without evidence, that he, rather than Joe Biden, had won the 2020 election. He urged the crowd to go to the Capitol to prevent Vice President Mike Pence from counting the votes of the Electoral College that would confirm the election of Joe Biden as president. With his provocative rhetoric, Donald Trump transformed the rally into a violent, angry human wave that inundated the Capitol in a bloody attack that threatened the lives of members of congress, including the vice president and the Speaker of the House. The attack brutalized and eventually killed members of the Capitol Police Force that tried to protect those members of

17. Allen, "Pulitzers Honor Darnella Frazier."
18. Jenkins, "Fatal Police Shootings."
19. Arkin, "Exclusive: Classified Documents Reveal."

Congress. The US House Select Committee to Investigate the January 6th Attack on the United States Capitol has made criminal referrals regarding the actions of the president to the Department of Justice.

Donald Trump refused to call off the people who had violently and angrily descended on the Capitol. He refused until his balking became untenable. What was at stake? The defense of Whiteness, of White power, of White superiority. The protection and advancement of Whiteness had been the hallmark of his presidency. In the October 2017 issue of *The Atlantic*, Ta-Nehisi Coates names Trump "The First White President" and says that Whiteness is "at the very core of his power." He ends his essay with this: "The first white president in American history is also the most dangerous president—and he is made more dangerous still by the fact that those charged with analyzing him cannot name his essential nature, because they too are implicated in it."[20] Coates wrote this assessment of Trump more than three years before Trump's followers swarmed the Capitol trying to stop the counting of electoral votes.

THE SUPREME COURT DECISION OVERTURNING ROE V. WADE

On June 22, 2022, in Dobbs v. Jackson, the conservative majority of the United States Supreme Court overturned the historic Roe v. Wade decision that has for almost fifty years protected the right of women to have an abortion. The Human and Civil Rights Clinic at The Howard University School of Law wrote an amicus brief in this case, supporting the appeal by Jackson Women's Health Organization to protect the Roe v. Wade decision. They wrote the brief "to place Mississippi's attempt to restrict abortion access within the historical context of state regulation of Black women's procreative liberty."[21]

---

20. Coates, "First White President."

21. Dobbs v. Jackson Women's Health Organization, 597 U. S. Supreme Court (2022), Howard Amicus, 2.

The Howard University School of Law amicus brief contends that overturning Roe v. Wade harms Black women more than any other group. How?

> Today, Black women are three to four times more likely to die during or after childbirth than white women. They are also more likely to experience "near misses"—barely escaping death—during and after delivery. Of these deaths and near misses, almost half result from preventable causes. And this heightened risk exists regardless of social, economic, or education level. "Put simply, for black women far more than for white women, giving birth can amount to a death sentence."[22]

The authors of this amicus brief place this decision in the historical context of the way Black women's ability to bear children has been exploited and abused. It has been so since the kidnapping of Black women who were brought to the Virginia colony in 1619. This history of abuse is founded on the dehumanization of Black people and in this case particularly Black women. African women were raped by White ship's officers in the voyage from Africa to the American colonies. They were sold and taken to plantations where they became victims of sexual abuse by their masters. They had no power to refuse sexual relations with the men who owned them.

After Congress prohibited the importation of slaves in 1808, slave masters could no longer replenish their labor force with slaves from abroad. Black women became valuable to their masters not only for their labor, but also for their ability to give birth—to more slaves. Thomas Jefferson once said, "I consider a slave woman who breeds once every two years as profitable as the best worker on the farm."[23] "The entirety of an enslaved Black woman's life was 'defined by her reduction to a sexual object, an object to be raped, bred, and abused.'"[24]

---

22. Dobbs v. Jackson Women's Health Organization, Howard Amicus, 18.
23. Dobbs v. Jackson Women's Health Organization, Howard Amicus, 6.
24. Dobbs v. Jackson Women's Health Organization, Howard Amicus, 6.

In Dobbs v. Jackson, the Supreme Court majority extended this abuse by handing down a decision that gives states permission to write laws that forbid all abortions without exceptions. The outcome of this legal arrangement is that in certain states a woman whose approaching childbirth is endangering her life must be denied an abortion. This decision affects every woman in that situation, but Black women are three to four times more likely than White women to die as a result.

These three events reveal the hidden and destructive power of Whiteness. Each event expresses the determined quest to protect and preserve Whiteness in this nation. The first is a police killing of an unarmed Black person that is one of hundreds of such murders that continue unabated despite efforts to change the police culture in this country. The second is a mob descending on the United States Capitol to carry out the wishes of a defeated president whose entire administration has been an attempt to defend, protect, and extend White supremacy. And the third is a Supreme Court decision against the right to abortion, the consequences of which will fall most heavily on Black women—women whose rates of infant and maternal mortality far exceed those of White women.

A NEW KEY IN THEOLOGICAL EDUCATION

Each of these three events gives us good reasons for developing a new key in theological education. That new key calls attention to experience that cannot be put into words, cannot be expressed in what Langer called *discursive symbolism*. These three events have in common one form of *presentational symbolism*—Whiteness.

I first began to recognize this new key several months after I completed the first draft of this manuscript, which I had titled "The Inner Textbooks of Students and Their Teachers." In that manuscript, I contended that in addition to the textbooks assigned for a class, students bring a textbook that's within themselves. It's their inner understanding of themselves and their world. For teaching to be effective, I contended, it must help students open up and examine their inner textbooks.

I had set out to find a publisher for the book. Then came the murder of George Floyd followed by my participation in a six-week workshop on "What Does It Mean to be White?" led by Rev. Benjamin Boswell, pastor of Myers Park Baptist Church in Charlotte, North Carolina. In the introduction to this workshop Boswell wrote,

> This curriculum amplifies the words and creativity of black leaders, intellectuals, and artists. . . . In the words of James Baldwin, "White people are trapped in a history they don't understand and until they understand it they cannot be released from it." Layla F. Saad says, "We cannot dismantle what we cannot see, or challenge what we don't understand." Therefore, as white people, learning to see and understanding the history and reality of whiteness is where our journey of becoming anti-racist begins.[25]

"We cannot dismantle what we cannot see." I had not seen the Whiteness of my manuscript, nor could I see that my manuscript had left out the four-hundred-year history of slavery, of Jim Crow oppression, and of the systemic oppression of Black people today. I wasn't paying attention to the deep scar of slavery that marked and distorted all of American history. I had not addressed the cultural and political storm that was brewing and that broke into the open with the election of Donald Trump as president and the mobilization of that office in the service of White supremacy. I saw that theological education cannot ignore the issue of race because it is deeply woven into all our lives.

I was concerned about racial oppression and had been active in advocating racial justice, which will be apparent in my story about being pastor of a southern church during the racial turmoil of the late sixties. At that time, I became involved in a community organization for improving race relations; however, I didn't recognize the

---

25. This workshop was part of a doctor of ministry research project which became a larger educational program with this participant's guide: Boswell, *Confronting Whiteness*.

racial problem within myself. I didn't understand the depth of my White privilege. I was not aware of my Whiteness.

WHITENESS AS PROPERTY

While I was pastor of that congregation in Gainesville, Florida, I got a lesson on Whiteness that I finally came to understand more than fifty years later. Here is what happened.

Fred was the Black custodian at Parkview Baptist Church where I was pastor in the late 1960s. I had given my resignation as pastor because my family and I were moving to Enid, Oklahoma, where I was joining the faculty of Phillips Theological Seminary.[26] I had told Fred that we were going to sell our second car, and he said he would like to buy it. We agreed on a price, and he went to the bank the next day to get a loan to pay for the car. He came back from his bank visit to tell me that he could not get a loan unless a White person co-signed the note. I wish I knew exactly what the bank loan officer had told him. Perhaps it was this: "Bank regulations don't let me make a loan to you. To get this loan you need to have a White person co-sign the note." Whatever they told Fred, this was, in fact, their message.

I co-signed the note, and Fred got the loan, but not without a dose of humiliation because his signature wasn't enough to secure the loan. Fred set about to purchase a car, a piece of property, but he couldn't do it until he produced another piece of property, called collateral. The particular form of that collateral property was not stated in the note, nor did anyone mention it. For it was invisible. *The collateral property that I provided was my Whiteness. My Whiteness had cash value.*

How can you call Whiteness property when it's invisible? It may be invisible, but as my story of selling the car to Fred reveals, the law recognizes Whiteness as property.

---

26. When I taught at this school, it was named The Graduate Seminary of Phillips University, and it was located in Enid, Oklahoma. Its name today is Phillips Theological Seminary, and it is located in Tulsa, Oklahoma.

In the June 1993 *Harvard Law Review*, Cheryl Harris wrote an article with the title "Whiteness as Property" in which she said, "Whiteness at various times signifies and is deployed as identity, status, and property, sometimes singularly, sometimes in tandem."[27] The legal understanding of Whiteness as property is rooted in "the commodification of human beings" who were slaves. "Slavery as a system of property facilitated the merger of white identity and property." The system of the enslavement of people because they were Black and the treatment of Black people as property led to the identification of Whiteness as property. "Whiteness was the characteristic, the attribute, the property of free human beings."[28] I went to the bank with Fred and put my signature on his loan document, thereby giving the bank my property of Whiteness to secure his loan.

I value my twenty-one years of teaching at Southeastern Baptist Theological Seminary and, before that, my five years of teaching at Phillips Theological Seminary. I led the Southeastern faculty to defend the school and its academic freedom from trustees who set about to make it an institution of biblical inerrancy. It was at Southeastern that I developed the teaching method I describe in the rest of this book. My life has been enriched by the relationships I have had with students and faculty.

However, when you have an all-White faculty, an all-White administration, and with few exceptions, an all-White student body; and when you live in a multi-racial and multicultural society; and when this society has been for four hundred years stained by racism with roots in 250 years of slavery; and when the foundations of the wealth of this nation were built on the labor of Black slaves, you have to ask, "Why were faculty members—including me—unable to see the utter Whiteness of the school?" That question has led me to rewrite this book.

I write this from my perspective as a White male, but I do not intend it to be read only by White persons. I invite people of color to read it as well and to consider how I have understood or failed to

---

27. Harris, "Whiteness as Property," 1725.
28. Harris, "Whiteness as Property," 1720–21.

understand their experience. I hope, in fact, that this book may be used by groups or classes of Black and White people together. I hope it will facilitate conversations about the personal experiences of participants as they have navigated their lives in the landscape of race.

THE THREE KEYS OF NARRATIVE, BELONGING AND DIVERSITY IN THE PARABLE OF THE GOOD SAMARITAN

Just then a lawyer stood up to test Jesus. "Teacher," he said, "what must I do to inherit eternal life?" He said to him, "What is written in the law? What do you read there?" He answered, "You shall love the Lord your God with all your heart, and with all your soul, and with all your strength, and with all your mind; and your neighbor as yourself." And he said to him, "You have given the right answer; do this, and you will live." But wanting to justify himself, he asked Jesus, "And who is my neighbor?"

Jesus replied, "A man was going down from Jerusalem to Jericho, and fell into the hands of robbers, who stripped him, beat him, and went away, leaving him half dead. Now by chance a priest was going down that road; and when he saw him, he passed by on the other side. So likewise a Levite, when he came to the place and saw him, passed by on the other side. But a Samaritan while traveling came near him; and when he saw him, he was moved with pity. He went to him and bandaged his wounds, having poured oil and wine on them. Then he put him on his own animal, brought him to an inn, and took care of him. The next day he took out two denarii, gave them to the innkeeper, and said, 'Take care of him; and when I come back, I will repay you whatever more you spend.'

Which of these three, do you think, was a neighbor to the man who fell into the hands of the robbers?" He said, "The one who showed him mercy." Jesus said to him, "Go and do likewise."[29]

---

29. Luke 10:25–37.

Jesus' audience identifies with this Jewish man who is traveling from Jerusalem to Jericho and gets robbed and beaten until he's almost dead. A priest comes down the road and avoids passing near the bleeding victim. Next comes a Levite, a temple assistant, and he, too, bypasses the injured man. The usual formula in such a narrative would be a priest, a Levite, and then the audience would expect an Israelite, a Jewish layperson. But the person who appears next is the last person they would want or expect to see. He's a Samaritan. Jewish disdain for Samaritans is encapsulated in a proverb that says that a Jew who eats the bread of the Samaritans is like one who eats the flesh of swine.[30] "From the Persian period in the late sixth century BCE to the time of Jesus, Jews and Samaritans remained at odds. Each claimed the true descent from Abraham, true understanding of Torah, the correct priesthood, and the right form of worship in the right location."[31] Two countries that shared the same border and couldn't abide each other. It's like Protestants and Catholics in Northern Ireland. It's like Jews and Palestinians in Israel.

Yet this hated Samaritan does not hesitate to go to the side of the bleeding, half-dead Jewish man. The rest of the parable tells in detail how this Samaritan dresses the wounds of the victim, takes him to an inn, pays for his lodging, and promises a follow-up visit. The story subverts the long-standing hatred and suspicion of Jews toward their Samaritan neighbors. It turns that conflict on its head with a narrative about a hated Samaritan rescuing and caring for a half-dead Jew.

Luke uses the parable as a moral example story, and that's the meaning typically given to the story, that this is what it means to be a good neighbor. Actually, the parable isn't about neighborliness at all. It's an earthquake underneath the years of Jews hating Samaritans. It's a subversive story that undermines a theology of purity that has fed years of hatred.

The parable is about Jews protecting their particular Jewish purity. What, we must ask, are our ways of protecting and defending

---

30. Scott, *Hear Then the Parable*, 197.
31. Levine, *Short Stories by Jesus*, 98.

our Whiteness? The legacy of White supremacy belongs to us, and it's up to us to do something about it.

Black/White diversity, more than any other form of social diversity, is a threat to the status quo of White supremacy in this country. The fortress of White supremacy is constructed to prevent diversity from contaminating the sacred treasure of Whiteness.

This parable is a narrative and, like the narrative of *Adventures of Huckleberry Finn*, it lays bare the truth of racial prejudice without trying to explain it. The story carries the meaning. It is truth with such nakedness that the gospel writer attempts to convert it into a moral example story.

And the parable is a story of belonging so intimate and compelling that it undermines racial prejudice as a hated enemy turns out to be the hearer's rescuer and healer.

CONCLUSION

Theological education in a new key
moves beyond our familiar words
to listen for the ineffable
that ordinary language
cannot express.

This theological education
tells and listens
to stories to convey
the substance of
what is being taught.

It invites students to
form strong bonds of
respect and affection with
their fellow students
and with their teachers.

It thrives on diversity—particularly
Black/White diversity—enjoying

the mutual understanding
these relationships can offer
and embracing the problems
and conflicts that this diversity
most likely will create.

It challenges the fortress
of White supremacy—
its ideology,
its exclusivism,
its destructive power.

Theological education in a new key
is led by the spirit and wisdom of Jesus
who challenged the oppression of a peasant society,
and awakened the peasants to
their value in God's eyes;
who healed those sick in body, mind, and spirit, and
who told parables that revealed
the duplicity of their oppressors
and the hope for their liberation.

2

Called to Be a Pastor in a Time of Racial Conflict

In the summer of 1967 I completed my graduate work, and my wife, Beverly, and I moved to Gainesville, Florida, with our infant son John. I became pastor of Parkview Baptist Church, a small suburban congregation.

The pastor search committee told us that the church had "dealt with the race issue" by deciding to accept African Americans into church membership—should any seek to join. Their acceptance, however, depended on the church determining that African Americans' request was genuine, that is, that they were not joining as a way to test the church's openness. White persons, on the other hand, didn't have to be interviewed. I could have been curious about this policy. What was the concern or fear that led to this decision? What did this policy say about the view of Black people held by the White members of the church? I had reservations about this policy, yet I did not press the issue. And I accepted at face value the assurance by members of the committee that the church membership believed in equality between Black people and White people. I was to learn that this gesture of apparent racial openness did not reflect the actual racial attitudes of the congregation.

A NATION'S RACIAL CONFLICT IN THE SUMMER OF 1967

We arrived in Florida just as racial conflict was breaking out in fourteen major US cities. That conflict occurred in Newark on July 12, 1967, when police arrested an African American taxi driver, dragging him from his cab, beating him, and taking him to a police station. Hundreds of people in a large housing project saw this happen and a crowd began to gather. Then a rumor spread that the taxi driver had died (which wasn't true). People began throwing bricks and Molotov cocktails. Fires erupted. And police charged at rioters. The state's governor called up the National Guard to quell the disturbance. In total, twenty-six people died, more than seven hundred were injured, and 1,500 were arrested. An even more lethal conflict occurred in Detroit on July 23. It was so severe that people in the community remembered it as the Rebellion of 1967. There, forty-three people died, the majority of them Black, 342 were injured, and more than 7,000 were arrested.[1]

Nationally, these events saturated the news. Locally, my family and I were moving into a city that had its own history of racial injustice. Gainesville is the Alachua County seat. Research authorized by the county commission had found that forty-six persons were known to have been lynched in Alachua County—all but four of them Black. And unreported lynchings surely added to this number. The last known lynching took place in 1926.[2]

The Alachua County School District did not fully integrate its schools until 1969 70, doing so only under court order. Students were distributed in each school in proportions that reflected the racial distribution in the county—70 percent White and 30 percent Black.[3]

---

1. Walsh, "50 Years After."
2. Swirko, "Alachua County Confronts."
3. Sloane, *Diminishing Barrier*.

Called to Be a Pastor in a Time of Racial Conflict

RACIAL CONFLICT AND GOD'S JUSTICE

Within a month of assuming my duties as pastor, with the racial conflict consuming the news, I decided I had to address this crisis. On August 6, 1965, I preached a sermon, "The Riots and God's Justice" drawing on the prophet Amos. I said that in the riots we were witnessing God's judgment, a judgment that occurs when justice toward African Americans is denied. I said that Amos believed that God cares supremely for every human being and that God depends on us to keep God's stream of justice open so it may flow out to everyone. When we reject the task of keeping the stream of justice open, the waters become heaped up until God's justice is made into judgment and the backed up waters tumble down and destroy. We are now witnessing that judgment—that's what these riots are telling us, I said. Further, Amos spoke for God, telling his audience, "I hate, I despise your feasts, and I take no delight in your solemn assemblies. . . . Take away from me the noise of your songs; to the melody of your harps I will not listen, but let justice roll down like waters, and righteousness like an ever-flowing steam."[4]

I believed that poverty was at the heart of this racial unrest, and I said that God is calling us not only to care for the poor but also to learn from the poor what it means for us to get in touch with our own spiritual poverty. Our spiritual poverty is revealed in our blindness to the plight of people who do not enjoy our White privilege, and we do not allow ourselves to be touched by their suffering. "Blessed are you poor," Jesus said, "for yours is the kingdom of God."[5] The poor know their need for God's intervention, for God's help. To learn from them is to be awakened to our deep need for God—a need that is hidden by our privilege and plenty.

I was told that at the end of the sermon the wife of the man who had chaired the pastoral search committee looked at him inquiringly, and he responded, "Marvelous!" Others were also affirming. I did not hear from those who opposed what I said.

---

4. Amos 5:21–24.
5. Luke 6:20.

MISUSE OF THE WORD "RIOTS"

My use of the word "riots" in my sermon fails to convey accurately what has occurred in these civil disturbances. It obscures the reality of years of racial oppression, and it tends to place the blame for these disturbances on Black people, or it implies that "both sides" are responsible for the causes of the unrest. It fails to recognize legitimate Black protests arising from their suffering under White domination, and it fails to convey the fact that the causes of "racial riots" are rooted in White oppression. In such disturbances some African Americans have responded with violence to years of racial oppression they have suffered, but to focus on their behavior as the center of the events hides the justifiable expression of distress born of racial oppression.

The Greenwood section of Tulsa, Oklahoma, was a thriving Black business community. In fact, it was so successful it was known as Black Wall Street. On May 31–June 1, 1921, this prosperous community was virtually destroyed in a concerted White attack. The attack laid waste to thirty-five square blocks of this prosperous, thriving African American community, and it left an estimated three hundred of its citizens dead.

As it approached the one-hundredth anniversary of this massacre, the state of Oklahoma formed the "1921 Tulsa Race Riot Commission" to investigate the White massacre in the Black community of Greenwood. In 2018, the chair of the Commission, State Senator Kevin Matthews, announced that the commission had decided to change its name to "the 1921 Race Massacre Commission." Matthews made this announcement in a news conference in which he said, "The fact that it was called a riot was one of the reasons given for turning down insurance claims." Citing other reasons for the name change, Matthews said, "The feelings and interpretation of those who experienced this devastation as well as current area residents and historical scholars have led us to more appropriately change the name to the 1921 Race Massacre Commission."[6]

---

6. Oklahoma Historical Society, "1921 Tulsa Race Massacre."

Formation of this commission prompted poet Steve Light to write an essay "Why 'Race Riot'? On the Need to Change a Misleading Term" in which he said,

> Why then did the massacres that took place in Tulsa, in Rosewood, in Atlanta and in other localities come to be depicted as "race riots" . . . usage of the term "race riot" *willfully* blurred the specifics of the events, and by this very blurring of specificity, had the precise effect, the precise function of removing blame, of shifting the blame away from the perpetrators of these attacks and massacres. Which race, whose race? And *who* is rioting? . . . What is being done and in what manner and to whom? All is left in doubt, all is left muddled in the term "race riot."

Steve Light's essay was consistently rejected by publications from 1997 until 2016 when it was finally published by the blog of the *Los Angeles Review of Books*.[7]

MARTIN LUTHER KING JR. IS ASSASSINATED

Less than a year after our arrival in Gainesville, on April 4, 1968, Martin Luther King Jr. was assassinated. The following Sunday I preached a sermon about the prophetic leadership of King to a congregation in which many saw him not as a prophetic figure but as a troublemaker. I drew from King's 1963 letter from Birmingham Jail:

> Perhaps it is easy for those who have never felt the darts of segregation to say, "wait." But when you have seen vicious mobs lynch your mothers and fathers at will and drown your sisters and brothers at whim; when you have seen hate-filled policemen curse, kick and even kill your black brothers and sisters; when you see the vast majority of your twenty million Negro brothers smothering in an airtight cage of poverty in the midst of an affluent society; when you suddenly find your tongue twisted and your speech stammering as

---

7. Light, "Why 'Race Riot'?," emphasis original. An extensive essay on the misuse of "riot" to describe the white massacre of Blacks in Tulsa, Oklahoma, is written by Marshall, "Tulsa Race Massacre."

you seek to explain to your six-year-old daughter why she can't go to the public amusement park . . . and see tears welling up in her eyes when she is told that Funtown is closed to colored children, and see ominous clouds of inferiority beginning to form in her little mental sky, and see her beginning to distort her personality by developing an unconscious bitterness toward white people . . . when your first name becomes "nigger," your middle name becomes "boy" . . . and your last name becomes "John," and your wife and mother are never given the respected title "Mrs."; when you are harried by day and haunted by night by the fact that you are a Negro . . . when you are forever fighting a degenerating sense of "nobodyness"—then you will understand why we find it difficult to wait.[8]

I concluded the service by inviting members of the congregation to join me and my wife in a Martin Luther King Jr. memorial march that afternoon. One lone church member joined us. Later on a church member reported another member telling him, "When he announced that he and his wife would be in that memorial march, my heart just sank!" His words no doubt reflected the feelings of many in that congregation.

THERE'S MORE THAN ONE BLACK COMMUNITY

Speaking from her perspective and research as a Black minister, Rev. Mia McClain read this manuscript and helped me to see that there is not one Black community; rather there are black communities—plural. She said,

> There is no one Black community. "The Black Community" is not a monolith, and I've found it necessary—even as a Black person in this country—to be specific about which Black community I'm talking about. . . . There were many Black communities who felt the same as your church members in Florida at the time—they hated Martin and Malcolm, just like they hated James Cone and other Black prophetic

---

8. King, *I Have a Dream*, 88.

voices who were disrupting the status quo. . . . I feel that it was a certain brand of Blackness you were interacting with.[9]

MY INTRODUCTION TO THE MOST VISIBLE BLACK COMMUNITY

Mt. Carmel Baptist Church was the final destination of that MLK memorial march at which civil rights activists spoke to an overflow crowd. Rev. Thomas A. Wright was pastor of Mt. Carmel. He was a well-known African American civil rights leader and president of the county NAACP. Tom and I became friends, and he helped me become acquainted with other African American ministers in the city. Our friendship included Beverly and me also getting to know Tom's wife, Affie. This friendship led to a cooperative relationship between members of our church and members of Mt. Carmel. Wright secured grants that enabled him and his church to develop a low-rent apartment complex, Gardenia Gardens, and members of our church helped move people into these new quarters.

At that time I did not know that three years earlier Wright had led a group of parents in the African American community to sue the Alachua County school board to integrate the county schools.

What had happened was this: prior to the beginning of the 1964–65 school year, testing a freedom-of-choice desegregation plan, parents of fifteen Black students requested transfers to what were then exclusively white schools. The school board denied their requests. Tom Wright and other Black leaders approached the school board to ask for voluntary integration before they would file suit for the schools to integrate. The school board refused. Following Wright's leadership, on July 2, 1964, the parents of fourteen students filed a class action suit to mandate the reorganization of the county's school

---

9. Mia McClain was associate minister of faith formation and outreach at Myers Park Baptist Church, Charlotte, North Carolina, when she read this manuscript. At this writing, she serves as the senior pastor of Riverside Baptist Church in Washington, DC, where she is the first African American and first woman to serve in that role in the church's 165-year history.

system into a "unitary nonracial system." This lawsuit remained active for fourteen years.[10]

Rev. Thomas Wright had moved to Gainesville from St. Augustine, Florida, and wanted to avoid the conflict he had faced there. His brother warned him that Gainesville was one of the headquarters of the Ku Klux Klan in Florida. Because Wright's reputation preceded him, soon after his arrival he was asked to serve as president of the local NAACP chapter. He agreed to lead it for six months. He ended up serving in that role for seventeen years.[11]

The school board opposed the lawsuit contending that it had adopted a freedom-of-choice system of integration and was not operating a segregated system. The NAACP lawsuit disagreed, seeking a unitary school system. In May 1968 in other litigation the Supreme Court put an end to the use of choice-based plans to satisfy constitutional standards. However, the Alachua County school board continued to operate under freedom-of-choice desegregation plans until 1970.[12]

After winning the court order for the integration of the county schools, Wright made every effort to get African American families to enroll their students in Gainesville High School. He was distraught because although he had enlisted a tenth and an eleventh grader, he had failed to sign up a high school senior.

Wright's daughter LaVon was a rising high school senior that year, and she saw her father's distress. After a long inner struggle, she volunteered to do it—to enroll in all-white Gainesville High School. She began classes in the fall of 1965. She tells this story in her book *Beyond Bravery*:

> When I entered my first classroom . . . immediately students in the entire first, second and third rows stood up, moving to the other side of the room. . . . All day, every day, no one spoke. These days of silence became a way of life, but I knew what else to expect. Each day some white boy or girl would

10. Gengler, *We Can Do It*, 67–68.
11. Gengler, *We Can Do It*, 69.
12. Gengler, *We Can Do It*, 67–75.

> spit on me and call me nigger. . . . Then one day, after my father dropped me off, a white boy jumped me in the school yard. His friends joined in. They beat me. They kicked me. They stomped me. . . . When I thought it was safe, I stumbled in the principal's office. I told him that I had been attacked and that I needed to get to the hospital. He said, "How did I know that you did not come to school bloody from your home? I did not see anyone mistreat you."

Finally she went to a pay phone and called her father. He took her to the only Black doctor in Gainesville. After days of recovery she was determined to return to the school. "I still carry scars," she said in an interview over fifty years later. "Time has not yet healed all of them. Despite the horror, I became the first Black student to graduate from Gainesville High School in 1965. I refused to give up then. I refuse to give up now. The struggle continues."[13] It would appear that LaVon's abusive treatment at Gainesville High School was payback for her father's engagement in a lawsuit against the county school board.

We arrived in Gainesville only two years after her torturous year at Gainesville High School, but I did not know this story until I read Dr. LaVon Bracy's recent account of her experience. Moreover, I am confident that at that time the White people of Alachua County, including the members of my church, did not know this story. Where would it have been told or published in the White community?

WORKING WITH THE BLACK COMMUNITY AGAINST RACIAL OPPRESSION

In the aftermath of King's death, a rising tide of concern for justice led an interracial group of citizens to form the Coordinating Council of Concern of Gainesville to deal with poverty and race relations. To my surprise, and the consternation of some members of my church, I was appointed chair of the Committee on Racial Discrimination.

I wondered just how I would proceed as chair of this committee. I didn't have to wait long. Mr. John Tucker, I shall call him, came

---

13. Bracy, "I Integrated Gainesville High."

to ask for my help. Tucker was an African American barber who worked at Sunland Training Center,[14] a large state facility in Gainesville for people with developmental disabilities. He told me that the administration of the institution had for years been taking advantage of Black employees. Among the grievances he reported were that White employees got promotions that Black employees had applied for and clearly deserved. They were consistently passed over. He told me about the supervisor of the cafeteria who made loans to Black employees, charging exorbitant interest, and then taking what they owed him out of their paychecks before distributing their salaries.

I said I was willing to help but that I would need documentation of these and other abuses in order to find a way to put a stop to them. Tucker agreed and over several weeks he secured extensive evidence of discrimination. He did this at considerable personal risk. This activity could have cost him his job or led to his arrest. I would call his action heroic.

In an astonishing political development, Claude Kirk, the first Republican governor of Florida since Reconstruction, appointed Jake Gaither the African American football coach at Florida A&M University to be his emissary to travel the state to find situations where there was racial tension that the governor should act upon. We arranged a meeting with Coach Gaither, and Tucker persuaded about eight Sunland employees to come and tell the governor's emissary their stories. At the end of the meeting we presented him with our notebook of evidence detailing racist employee abuses at the school. At that time I did not know that Coach Gaither was a legendary Black coach and a civil rights activist as well.[15]

A few weeks later I got a call from Tucker, who reported changes that enabled Black employees to get the promotions they deserved, that the supervisor of the cafeteria had been fired, and that the institution's grievance committee now had a Black member. The changes were not grand ones, but they were steps in the right direction. The

---

14. Curry, *Sunland Training Centers*.
15. D'Angelo, Review of *Blood, Sweat, and Tears*; White, *Blood, Sweat, and Tears*.

stranglehold of White supremacy had been, if not broken, at least loosened.

AN INTERRACIAL PULPIT EXCHANGE: THE LAST STRAW

On another front, I made arrangements for an interracial pulpit exchange with a Black Methodist pastor. This seemed to me a modest move toward interracial understanding. In a deacons' meeting soon after this announcement I heard that, as one of the deacons put it, "An alarming number of people are upset about this pulpit exchange!" His statement troubled me because he was among my strongest supporters. A few minutes later the deacon chair, along with another deacon, resigned in protest of the pulpit exchange and walked out of the meeting.

After the meeting, one of the younger deacons called me aside and, referring to the "alarming number of people" statement, said, "Dick, you need to remember that Fred's wife, Nell, can herself become an alarming number of people." Nonetheless, over several months that alarming number did become about sixty people who left our already small congregation in response to my efforts to challenge racial injustice in the community. The interracial pulpit exchange went ahead as planned. The Methodist pastor preached at Parkview, and a few weeks later I preached at his church and received a warm welcome.

I myself left Parkview Baptist Church at the beginning of 1970 when I received a faculty appointment at Phillips Theological Seminary in Enid, Oklahoma.

I learned recently that sometime in the mid-1970s Rev. Wright was asked to exchange pulpits with the new minister at Parkview Baptist. The *Gainesville Sun* had published an announcement of the exchange in its church section the preceding Saturday. That night Wright's phone rang and the caller told him he would be killed if he showed up at Parkview. Parkview was informed of the threat. Wright's son, Philoron, drove his parents to the church. Rev. Wright tells that upon his and his wife's arrival "they had young men in dark suits on each side of the walk, and as we marched down the walk to go into the church, they said, 'Welcome, Reverend and Mrs. Wright, to Parkview.' I went in. An assistant minister conducted the service. I preached. And when I got through preaching at Parkview, I didn't see a dry eye in that church." Philoron had parked across the street with a pistol in his lap watching for anyone who might try to make good on the threat of the night before. No one appeared.[16]

THE ONGOING INFLUENCE OF THE GAINESVILLE EXPERIENCE

What happened in Gainesville from 1967 to 1970 decisively shaped my commitment to social justice. In Gainesville I stepped out of my all-White past and into a world of racial diversity. Those who suffered under the White supremacy structures of the South gave me a first-hand education on racial injustice. The people in the all-White Parkview Baptist Church who suffered from the fear of personal encounter with Black people as their equals—fear produced by White supremacist propaganda against African Americans—also educated me. Before coming to this church I had never been the target of the fear and anger people felt about relating to Black people as equals. This fear and anger forced me to decide: Would I speak out against racial injustice, or would I retreat because I feared the White anger in the congregation? I couldn't retreat—and I didn't.

I did not have a clear understanding of the congregation's and community's anxiety about race. To bring about the change for which I hoped, I needed to have spent more time with members, getting to know them better than I did and learning to understand their view of the world. I particularly needed to do this with members who disagreed with me.

I took actions toward racial justice without necessarily consulting with the leadership of the congregation. This was a congregationally governed Baptist church. It required that I work within

16. Gengler, *We Can Do It*, 408–9.

a democratic process. This is not to say that I would confine my preaching, teaching, and community involvement to what was acceptable to the majority. It says that I needed to engage the congregational leadership and encourage them to express their opinions. I needed to tell them why I was taking a particular course of action and invite them to challenge me. I don't at all regret the things I did as an advocate for racial equality. But the way I did it left room for improvement.

From my experience with the Black employees at Sunland, I received a first-hand lesson in systemic racism. After I first heard the complaints about racial discrimination at Sunland from Mr. Tucker, two other White clergy colleagues and I went to meet with the superintendent and assistant superintendent of that institution. We told of the complaints of discrimination we had received from their Black employees. They told us Black employees had never come to them with complaints, nor had they come to the center's grievance committee. "How many African Americans serve on the grievance committee?" we asked. "None," they told us. Nonetheless, they assured us that if there were real problems they would have heard about it. They led an institution steeped in racial injustice. Systemic racism expressed itself in their assumption that a grievance committee with only White people on it was neutral territory, and this being so, if Black employees had a grievance they would come to the committee.

LEAVING THE WORK OF RACIAL JUSTICE AND ENTERING THE ALL-WHITE ACADEMY

At Parkview Baptist I received my first education about racial justice, but I did not pursue this education when I began my seminary teaching career. And now I ask myself, "How did I lose sight of the problem of racial oppression as an urgent issue?" When I began teaching, I entered an all-White arena where I became insulated from the reality of racial oppression. Moreover, I did not yet have the knowledge I needed to view my situation from the perspective of White supremacy and my White privilege. I did, however, have one particular opportunity to re-enter the world of racial oppression.

During the time I was teaching at Phillips Theological Seminary the dean asked me to be the faculty advisor of a Black student who I shall call Wendell. He was the son of the president of an African American seminary. It seems that Wendell's father and my dean decided it would be a good idea to exchange seminary students for a year. Wendell's father sent him to Phillips and my dean sent one of our students to the Black seminary. Wendell wasn't interested in pursuing a theological education, and he came to our seminary under duress. He was there in body but not in spirit. He was understandably angry.

I tried my best to understand Wendell's situation and his anger about being sent here. I did not know what to do with him. To his credit, he set about to teach me about Enid's Black community. He persuaded me to go with him to visit Black nightclubs—being careful to warn me how dangerous this was. I went under his supervision and protection. He taught me about the conditions of poverty and suffering in the Black community as it existed in the shadow of White privilege. All this made me anxious. I was out of my comfort zone and like a fish out of water. I needed help to know how to relate to Wendell and what to do with what he was teaching me.

As I look back on it, I believe God gave me Wendell as a gift so I could continue the education in racial justice that had begun in Gainesville, Florida. I wasn't able to take that gift and, as we might say, run with it. Instead, I walked with it—slowly and uncertainly.

GAINESVILLE, FLORIDA, PARKVIEW BAPTIST CHURCH, AND THE AMERICAN CASTE SYSTEM

The racial caste system is a template that can be placed over my experiences as a pastor in Gainesville. Isabel Wilkerson, in her book *Caste: The Origins of Our Discontents* provides a searching description of the US caste system. She describes it this way:

> Like other old houses, America has an unseen skeleton, a caste system that is as central to its operation as are the studs and joists that we cannot see in the physical buildings we call home. Caste is the infrastructure of our divisions. It is the architecture of human hierarchy, the subconscious code of instructions for maintaining, in our case, a four-hundred-year-old social order. Looking at caste is like holding the country's X-ray up to the light.

A caste system, she says, uses rigid artificial boundaries to keep ranked groups separate from each other. This caste system endures because it is often supported by a theology that says it's part of the divine will. It is culturally reinforced and its structure is passed down through the generations. Caste is about power and resources—which caste deserves them and which caste doesn't. Caste guides us daily in ways that are outside our awareness. "It embeds into our bones an unconscious ranking of human characteristics and sets forth the rules, expectations, and stereotypes that have been used to justify brutalities against entire groups within our species. In the American caste system, the signal of rank is what we call race . . . the primary tool and visible decoy, the front man, for caste." She adds one more metaphor: "If we have been trained to see humans in the language of race, then caste is the underlying grammar that we encode as children, as when learning our mother tongue."[17]

- The prospect of integration of the Gainesville public schools threatened the White caste which was represented by the school board. Rev. Thomas Wright, president of the local NAACP, led the legal battle that breached this caste barrier. His daughter, LaVon Wright Bracy, experienced the hate-filled backlash of White students (and no doubt their parents) against her courageous, caste-breaking entry into the all-White Gainesville High School.
- I was pastor of an all-White congregation, and the natural inclination of the majority of the people in the congregation was to

---

17. Wilkerson, *Caste*, 17–18.

resist any activity that mixed White and Black people together. This resistance was expressed in many ways, perhaps the most open of which was the objection to my arranging an interracial pulpit exchange which visibly broke through caste barriers. This was a different caste transgression than having Black people visit the church or cooperating with members of a Black congregation. In a pulpit exchange, an African American minister speaking from the pulpit fills a place of authority and power, and for some this perceived inversion of authority and power, this public caste violation, was intolerable.

- A minority of members of the Parkview congregation wanted to cross the caste lines to work with African Americans. I believe they were motivated by their understanding of the Christian gospel of love for all humankind. And I believe my preaching and teaching contributed to their motivation for interracial cooperation. They wanted personally and deliberately to break through the caste barrier.

- The systemic preservation of caste was most evident in the county public school system and at Sunland Training Center. In both cases only a higher authority—the federal courts in the case of the public school system and the governor of Florida in the case of Sunland Training Center—overcame caste resistance. In each case the formal, *de jure* caste boundary was breached but the invisible power of the *de facto* boundary remained.

- One of the most important things I did in Gainesville was to lead members of Parkview Baptist Church in a cooperative endeavor with Rev. Tom Wright's Mt. Carmel Baptist Church. This effort was primarily *interracial*. We stepped beyond caste barriers to join forces with members of Mt. Carmel to help disadvantaged Black people move into subsidized housing. It would be safe to say that neither I nor the members of Parkview Baptist had an *intraracial* understanding—an understanding that we carried within ourselves a Whiteness that was the mark of our caste and

Called to Be a Pastor in a Time of Racial Conflict

- the legacy of four hundred years of White oppression of African Americans.
- Turning again to my relationship to Wendell; that relationship was difficult for me and for him because we were trying to meet each other in a caste system that was dedicated to keeping us apart, with me in a superior position of power and Wendell in an inferior position of power. Not only did Wendell have an inferior caste position, he did not have other Black companions to support him as he tried to negotiate his relationship to a White professor in an all-White seminary. He had been put into an impossible position. However, he sought relationships within his caste in the Black community of Enid. And he took me inside that caste to get a view of what it was like.

THE KEYS[18]

As I wrote this chapter, I could see layers of the story of the church and the community that I didn't see at the time I was a pastor there. Perhaps the most striking layer was the *narrative* about the July 2, 1964, lawsuit led by Rev. Thomas Wright for the integration of the county school system[19] and how the high school students and administration abused Rev. Wright's daughter LaVon when she enrolled in the twelfth grade—as the only Black senior.

Belonging is the issue at every turn of this story. Can White people belong with Black people in community and break out of caste confinement? Can Black persons belong at Parkview Baptist Church? Can Black persons enroll in the all-White county school system? Can members of Parkview Baptist Church and Mt. Carmel Baptist Church belong together to make a common effort to find ways to meet the needs of poor Black people? And by their departure,

---

18. I conclude this chapter and the following chapters by noting how the primary themes of the book appear in that chapter: narrative, belonging, diversity, and the ineffable. And the primary ineffable idea is Whiteness.

19. Gengler, *We Can Do It*.

were those who left the congregation expressing, "We don't belong in this church anymore?"

The county school board resisted *diversity*. As did the leaders at Sunland Training Center. And the most notable resistance to diversity I experienced came when I arranged an interracial pulpit exchange, and some people became very distressed to see a Black minister in our White pulpit. Diversity challenges caste.

Whiteness was not in my vocabulary until more than thirty years after I was pastor at Parkview Baptist Church. Throughout this story Whiteness is an unseen reality that shaped events. It is the unseen, the ineffable, power of White supremacy to preserve the racial status quo—in the school system, in Sunland Training Center, in responses to the interracial pulpit exchange.

QUESTIONS

1. What is your story of the development of your social justice ideas and actions?
2. What kinds of interracial relationships have you had, and how did they affect the way you see things?
3. What has been your introduction to the idea of "Whiteness" and your response to it?
4. Can you tell a story about the power of caste and how it affected you?

3

Early Childhood Memories and Jesus' Parables

THIS CHAPTER IS AN account of how three people—two of my students and myself—worked with an assignment to relate early childhood memories to a parable of Jesus. The following is how I articulated the semester assignment in the course "Theology and Self-Understanding":

> Identify your three earliest childhood memories and relate them to a parable of Jesus. As best you can, identify your age at the time of each memory. Select memories that have a story plot—not a memory snapshot. They are to be recollections of particular events—not something like "What we always did at Christmas." Use critical biblical resources to interpret the parable—those I have recommended and others. You will submit three drafts of the paper so that I can give you feedback along the way. As part of the class, you will meet with other students in a weekly small group session to share your work on this assignment and to have mutual support.

The students wrote these papers in the late 1980s and early 1990s. Between 2015 and 2018, I was able to have a telephone follow-up call with the two students whose papers I use in this chapter, and with others in that course, to learn whether this project had a lasting effect on them (and subsequently to ask their permission to use their stories here). I drafted my account of a parable and one of my early memories in December 2020, as I rewrote this manuscript after recognizing the Whiteness of it.

ALICE'S EARLY MEMORY, A PARABLE, AND A RECONCILIATION

Alice, a twenty-eight-year-old seminary student, writes of a painful conflict with her family that occurred when she was twenty-five. She had returned home to live with her parents "temporarily until I could get work, get on my feet." She went home for a refuge but found something else. She writes,

> One day my father took me aside and said, "Your sister's coming home from college soon; you'll have to find some place to stay." Soon after, my sister came home and moved into my old room. And unknown to me, she then began dating the man I was dating. They eventually married. I learned that fathers are capable of rejection and sisters are capable of deception. I learned that bad deeds are not always punished and good deeds are not always rewarded. And I learned that for all my good behavior, nothing could keep me from being displaced by my family, nothing could keep me from losing the safety I had so carefully developed for myself.
>
> I have attached myself to these memories and used them as an excuse to sever family ties. I have been obsessed by my own victimization and have seen myself as the wounded flower upon whom life has not smiled, despite all I did to deserve grand and wonderful treatment. My reluctance to forgive tells me that all did not begin with those events.
>
> My earliest memory is of stealing into my newborn sister's room and taking her baby bottle. I brought it with me into the dining room, conspicuously hid under the dining room table, and began to drink. The introduction of an intruder into the family midst forced me to reassess my position. No longer was I the privileged one. The baby demanded

priority. The displacement was impossible to bear, and so I planned to reverse it.[1]

Here, Alice sets the stage for the unfolding story of her childhood and early adulthood, her feelings of rejection by her parents, and her decision to cut off all ties to her family.

What about such early memories? I learned about the power of early memories from Alfred Adler (1870–1937), a psychoanalyst who was a contemporary of Sigmund Freud. Unlike Freud, he related to his patients as equals and gave attention to their social context. He asked new patients to tell him their earliest childhood memories. He created a psychological movement that emphasized a holistic view of individuals in their social context. His school of therapy is called Individual Psychology. His most influential concept was "social interest"—one's personal interest to foster the welfare of others through collaboration and cooperation.

Alice's reflection on her family situation reports her earliest childhood memory and shows how it is a paradigm for her place in the family as a young adult. Adler gave careful attention to early memories because he understood that our memory is highly selective and retains only what is consistent with our present style of life. When we look back on our past we make "an anthology of pictures and incidents," choosing only those that are congruent with the striving of our style of life.[2] "The more one is occupied with earliest childhood recollections," he said, "the more attractive the matter becomes. One hits upon relationships which show human nature in a shattering light."[3]

The "style of life" revealed in early memories consists of a constellation of private and largely unconscious goals that guide a person's perceptions, thought, and action. These personal constructs constitute the "private logic" of the person. "The beliefs that compose

---

1. The account of my work with this student first appeared in Hester, "Memory, Myth, Parable," 444–50. In Alice's class, I asked for one early childhood memory, not three as I did in later classes.
2. Adler, *What Life Should Mean*, 102.
3. Ansbacher and Ansbacher, *Alfred Adler*, 197.

the music of one's behavior are together—the composition and the music—the individual's life style."[4] Early memories aren't causally related to the present; rather our present style of life guides what early memories we admit into awareness. These early memories are compact versions of our current style of life.[5] I use the metaphor of an "inner textbook" to describe what Adler calls a person's "private logic." Alice's account illustrates how Adler's understanding of early memories plays itself out.

Alice worked to understand her early childhood memory in light of Jesus' parable of the wheat and tares (weeds):

> He put before them another parable: "The kingdom of heaven may be compared to someone who sowed good seed in his field; but while everybody was asleep, an enemy came and sowed weeds among the wheat, and then went away. So when the plants came up and bore grain, then the weeds appeared as well. And the slaves of the householder came and said to him, 'Master, did you not sow good seed in your field? Where, then, did these weeds come from?' He answered, 'An enemy has done this.' The slaves said to him, 'Then do you want us to go and gather them?' But he replied, 'No; for in gathering the weeds you would uproot the wheat along with them. Let both of them grow together until the harvest; and at harvest time I will tell the reapers, Collect the weeds first and bind them in bundles to be burned, but gather the wheat into my barn.'"[6]

Alice reports that at first she understood the parable as a perfect description of her life. She saw herself as the good seed in "an idyllic field of wheat." The enemy is her parents who sow the bad seed, her sister. The sister comes into the field and pollutes it. Like the slaves in the parable, Alice sees herself asking, "What shall I do? Can I get rid of her?" As she looks back on this conflict, she reconstructs how she saw things back then:

---

4. Manaster and Corsini, *Individual Psychology*, 15.
5. Powers, "Myth and Memory," 287.
6. Matt 13:24–30.

Early Childhood Memories and Jesus' Parables

> If I get rid of her, there might be unpleasant repercussions for me. I will deal with the problem another way. I will be patient and as time passes and as growth continues, I will force my parents, by my exemplary behavior, to see me for the good seed and to see my sister as the intruder weed. If I'm good enough, they will restore me to my state of former significance and justice will be done. The weeds will be bundled for burning and the wheat is returned to the safety and nurture of the barn.

Alice then describes the theology that grew out of and supported this lifelong quest to be the chosen one in her family.

> In my wishful thinking, I sought to give God the power to exact judgment for a wrong I felt had been done. As a child, I knew from experience that children get punished for doing wrong, for being bad; and they get rewarded for doing good. Therefore, it made sense that God would punish my sister, who was intrinsically bad by virtue of existence, and reward me because I was so obviously good.

Alice explored the critical research on this parable and discovered the early church's view of it as an apocalyptic judgment on the unrighteous and salvation for the righteous—a view similar to her own outlook. She also found an interpretation of the parable as a call to patience—leaving judgment to God. But then she found C. H. Dodd's interpretation of the parable as a warning against the quest for purity and a call to embrace ambiguity even in the midst of the coming of the kingdom of God.[7]

As I had invited all my students to do, Alice sought conferences with me as she got in touch with the pain of her story and its implications. As she put together the pieces of the puzzle of this educational process, her parable began to undermine her mythical world. She began to see a God she had not seen before. In the "progressively less judgment-oriented interpretations" of her parable, she writes, "lives a God I haven't seen before."

---

7. Dodd, *Parables of the Kingdom*.

> A God who requires that we see reality and live with it. The field of wheat has weeds in it. There is nothing to do but accept it and go on. I am a field of wheat with weeds in it, not just a field of wheat. My sister is a field of wheat with weeds in it, not just a crop of weeds. Life is a field of wheat with weeds in it. Reality. Can I look it in the eye? This new God seems to tell me that's required. By avoiding the weed reality, I close my eyes to life. By facing the weed reality, I honestly appraise what is there and find that without expectations of perfection I can appreciate the vast diversity which comes closest to approximating perfection.

She finds God saying, "Look at the field of wheat and weeds. Live with it; release the fantasy of purity and embrace the ambiguous reality you're living in."

Alice sees her own "dark manipulative side, a side that refused acceptance and tolerance of others and opted for a plan to eliminate the competition." She describes what has happened as her early childhood recollection connects with the parable:

> An old world view has been subverted and an incomplete one has taken its place, leaving me with the feeling that I am walking on the edge of a precipice, always unprotected, never knowing when I'm going to fall. This uncertainty throws me back to a faith in a God I barely know, in a self I barely know, in a world I've avoided for 28 years. Perhaps that's what it means to be born again.[8]

THE LEARNING ENVIRONMENT OF THE CLASS

I taught this "Theology and Self-Understanding" class for seven years, from 1984 to 1991, to a total of 478 students. This was an educational experiment. I hadn't done anything like it before. In the early semesters of the course I asked students to "Relate your earliest childhood memory to a biblical narrative." In those classes I discovered that those few who chose a parable of Jesus wrote papers that

---

8. Hester, "Memory, Myth, Parable," 449–50.

Early Childhood Memories and Jesus' Parables

showed more searching self-exploration than what was elicited by other biblical narratives. I then re-wrote the assignment to focus exclusively on the parables of Jesus. I also discovered that I should ask them to relate the parable to their three earliest memories—rather than limiting them to one early memory. Three memories gave them more narrative material to work with, and they could show how these memories interacted with each other and the parable.

Did the experiment work? Actually, it exceeded my expectations as evidenced by the many copies of student papers I have kept for thirty years. Those who wrote the papers I've kept gave me permission to use them in research and publication. Two of these papers frame this chapter.

What made this pedagogical experiment work?

WHEN MEMORY AND PARABLE INTERACT

The course assignment called on students to bring to a parable a highly personal narrative that provided a compact image of their present life. I shared with them at the beginning of the semester Alfred Adler's theory of the nature of early childhood memories and how these memories disclose one's present life story. At that point, however, it was only a theory, and they could not foresee what those early memories would tell them.

The assignment was to relate early childhood memories to a parable of Jesus, but what is the nature of this relationship? And what kind of power is released when parable and memory interact? Amy-Jill Levine, a Jewish rabbi and professor of New Testament, writes that parables

> tease us into recognizing what we've already always known, and they do so by reframing our vision. The point is less that they reveal something new than that they tap into our memories, our values, and our deepest longings, and so they resurrect what is very old, and very wise, and very precious. And often, very unsettling.[9]

9. Levine, *Short Stories by Jesus*, 22–23.

Levine's description resonates with the metaphor of inner textbooks as a place where parable can lead us to find, in the pages of our own experience, evidence of God's ceaseless attempts to get our attention.

Most of Jesus' parables are addressed to peasants in small Galilean villages. These peasants exist on life's barest necessities. Their relentless daily labor benefits wealthy landowners who oppress them with propaganda that tells them they're getting only what they deserve. Jesus' parables open the peasants' eyes to see the lie in the oppressors' claims that God ordained their social inferiority. At the same time, the parables open their eyes to see the value of their own culture and tradition and the often heroic acts they've taken to help themselves, their families, and their neighbors survive.

I was able to accompany students as they worked at relating their early childhood memories to one of Jesus' parables by asking them to submit three drafts of the paper. I responded to each draft with curiosity. I asked about possible connections between memories and parable—wondering whether this or that particular linkage was possible. And I noted where I saw a creative dialogue between parable and memory. I read these papers with anticipation because they were marked by personal risk, perplexity, and unexpected discovery. The students and I had a lively dialogue as I read and responded to their drafts.

The assignment required students to do research to learn what biblical scholarship had done with their parable. Leaders of the early church, including the Gospel writers, tamed Jesus' parables. They domesticated them by converting them into moral example stories or allegories or lessons. These domestications have continued in the church and in scholarly interpretations of the parables. In her account, Alice told how the parable of the wheat and tares had been tamed by making it into an apocalyptic scene of judgment which was meant to be a warning to wayward church members—not at all a narrative *against* the attempt to separate the "good" members from the "bad" ones. Alice came to an interpretation that depicts God as one who embraces the good and bad together and rejects attempts to purify the community of "bad" members. Such an understanding of the parable in the early centuries of the church was a threat to the authority of church leaders bent on a program of deciding who was in the fold and who wasn't. As students did critical research on their chosen parable, they often discovered the parable's subversive power. This sent them upstream against the historical tide of conventional interpretation that had domesticated their parable.

RACISM AND NOT GOING FAR ENOUGH UPSTREAM

Racism lies deep within *the historical tide of conventional interpretation that domesticates parables*. Not overt racism that would be easy to detect, but covert racism that is blind to the power of White privilege. What does it mean to read the interpretation of a parable in commentaries by White males who never mention race? Most of the commentaries I recommended made no mention of race as an issue that should be considered. And when I was teaching these seminary students I had not gone far enough upstream to recognize how racism influenced the interpretation of these parables.

Malu Fairley-Collins, a Black theological educator who has read this manuscript, told me, "I cannot read the parables and not read race in them." Her observation jolts me into a recognition that she and I view the Bible and the parables in particular with quite different lenses, and that calls upon me to pay attention to these different lenses. In *The Cross and the Lynching Tree*, James Cone, the founder of Black liberation theology, has this to say,

> The Newark and Detroit riots in July 1967 and the assassination of Martin Luther King, Jr. in April 1968 were the events that shook me out of my theological complacency, forcing me to realize the bankruptcy of any theology in America that did not engage the religious meaning of the African American struggle for justice. What I studied in graduate school ignored white supremacy and black resistance against it, as if they had nothing to do with the Christian gospel and the discipline of theology. Silence on both white supremacy and the black struggle against racial segregation made me angry with a fiery rage that had to find expression.

> How could any theologian explain the meaning of Christian identity in America and fail to engage white supremacy, its primary negation?[10]

In the previous chapter I told about my awakening to the urgency of the oppression of Black people and my sense of calling for me and for our congregation to address the problem. I was awakened by the same circumstances in 1967 that awakened James Cone—awakened him and awakened me to how our theological education had ignored White supremacy and the Black struggle against racial segregation. And there I was pastor of a suburban White congregation that was trying to protect itself from the fallout of the racial distress manifest in the Newark and Detroit expressions of racial oppression and in the assassination of Martin Luther King Jr. Out of his distress and awakening from these events Cone proceeded to develop Black liberation theology. I proceeded to accept a teaching position in an all-White seminary and joined the ranks of White male theologians. I became insulated from the Black experience and awareness of White supremacy. The one exception to my becoming a captive to White theological education was Wendell, the Black student who God sent to me as a messenger to challenge me to stay awake to the predicament of Black people. I deeply regret that I did not make the most of that remarkable gift.

RETURNING TO MY DESCRIPTION OF THE CLASS ON PARABLES AND EARLY MEMORIES

I hope that my uneven awareness of Black oppression and White supremacy will serve to awaken others to the way these issues have been suppressed in White theological education. I take up here where I left off in my description of the class on parables and early memories.

Each student belonged to a small group in the class. In those groups, participants entered into liminal space that was outside their usual way of study, work, and activity. They were on a personal

---

10. Cone, *Cross and the Lynching Tree*, xvi–xvii.

spiritual journey with companions who were engaged in the same challenging task.

The success of these groups depended on a skilled group facilitator who was also taking the course. I knew the facilitators from other classes, and I trusted them to be effective, empathic leaders. I met with these facilitators each week for a class on group process that focused on their facilitation of these groups. The facilitators and I made up a teaching team for the course. The groups provided a liminal container for supporting students as they explored their inner textbooks. I describe this teaching team and the groups in greater detail in chapter 6.

MY CONVERSATION WITH ALICE THIRTY YEARS LATER

Alice wrote her paper in 1986. Thirty years later I located her and talked with her about the class. I taught that class as a visiting professor at another seminary during a summer term. I did not have the time or resources to provide the small group component for that class. Actually, I did not know at the time how critical the small groups were. My conversation with Alice left no doubt.

I asked her, "What happened after you wrote the paper?" "The process of writing this paper subverted my world view," she said. "I came out of the class energized and not knowing what to do next. I was rattled because it felt like there was no firm reality any more. I felt kind of shattered." She said she found John Dominic Crossan's book *The Dark Interval*,[11] and it helped clarify what she was going through. His book comforted her because Crossan seemed to understand her perplexity and gave her a metaphor for her sense that she no longer had something solid under her feet. "He told a story about people on a raft in the ocean and they couldn't find land. All they had were the edges of the raft which to me represented the boundaries of my new world view." She continued,

> I was on a raft, and this brought a weird unsettlement into my life. It brought a darkness. It isn't a bad darkness, but it's

11. Crossan, *Dark Interval*.

a darkness that's a not knowing. It's the dark interval! It's chaos. It's a mystery and always the possibility that I couldn't predict or control what would happen. To find that out is sort of a spiritual devastation. It shook me to my core.

Later in her work as a therapist, she said, "I heard of Michael White's book, *Narrative Means to Therapeutic Ends*,[12] and I thought, 'This is it! This is exactly it!' Michael White's book was a comfort to me. It was like standing under a warm shower. God put that book in my path." The book affirmed her experience of being on a raft where she had only narrative to hold on to. And that was, in fact, an asset in her therapy practice. Following the practice of Michael White's narrative therapy, she could help her clients find an alternative narrative to the problem story that was giving them pain.

My conversation with Alice told me two things. The first was the power of the assignment that indeed made a difference in her life and subverted her world view of certainty. The second thing was how Alice suffered alone with the shattering of her world view. I had failed her because at that time I didn't understand how utterly essential the small groups were. I told Alice that I deeply regretted that I hadn't provided that support for her and the other students who needed a community where they could share their common experience and know they weren't alone on the raft. You will see in chapter 6 how the small groups in this and other courses I taught were as important as whatever I said and did in the full class sessions.

JEFF'S EARLY MEMORY, A PARABLE, AND A MURDER

Jeff tells this early memory:

> In my first memory (I'm almost five) my father interrupts my playing in my aunt's room to tell me my mother has died. He picks me up from the floor where I am playing with her paper dolls and sets me by him on the bed (or in his lap?) and tells me plainly she is dead. I don't remember his filling

---

12. White and Epston, *Narrative Means*. Chapter 7 in this book is my discussion of narrative therapy and Michael White's contribution to it.

me in on details or the like; I remember a focus on the future: We'll be all right, the three of us [Jeff, his father, and his younger brother]. I don't remember how/what I felt; I don't remember him crying. I have no recollection of my mother or of anything which occurred before this day.

In a second memory, he recalls that when he was five or six, he and his brother were involved in "a neighborhood 'war' in which children were arrayed on opposite sides of a big ditch across which they hurled dirt clods and more." He knew he shouldn't be there. He stood up and, he said, caught a brick in the side of the head. "I don't remember any blood and I don't remember the 'war' stopping on account of my casualty."[13]

His third recollection reports that "my family would go sailing in Ossabaw Sound" on weekends. He was seven and had just finished a series of swimming lessons. When swimming around the boat he had always worn a life vest and was tethered to the boat. This time, he said, "I'm going in on my own. My dad responds to my question about the depth of the water with the remark—intended I suppose as reassurance—that I could drown in four as easily as in forty feet of water. With this he pitches me over the side and I swim unassisted for the first time."

Following Alfred Adler's practice, he asks how these memories may reveal his current style of life. About the memory of the "war" he says,

> One thing that has remained constant in my recollection of this event is the impression that I was "in over my head." I was a precocious child and did not hesitate to dive into a situation and think about how to get out of it later. . . . Getting hit with the brick was not the first or last time I got caught where I shouldn't have been and it served less to discourage future excursions and more to cultivate a respect for secrecy

---

13. One would think that a five- or six-year-old boy getting hit in the head with a brick would have been life-threatening or even fatal. Most likely this did not actually happen. It is not unusual for such a distortion of reality to occur in an early memory. The question would be "Why?" He offers an answer to that in his subsequent reference to that event.

and alibi. My myth has included an aspect of immunity to getting caught short.

About this memory Jeff says further,

> One of the most emotionally powerful aspects of my life has been my recent exploration into (for me) uncharted theological and "metaphysical" reality. I have cut loose from customary moorings and pushed off determined to follow wherever my thought leads me. I don't have a plan for getting back or for putting back together what I'm tearing apart as I go along.

He does not elaborate on this statement. Given the overall content of his paper, this apparently means he has "cut loose" from the conventional theological wisdom with which he grew up.

About the memory of his dad pitching him over the side of the boat without a life jacket, he says, "I can't get my dad to admit it happened.... For my dad, it's important that I never went in without being tethered to the family boat. For myself, I must go in on my own even if I have to invent a history of such action." Here Jeff recognizes the malleability of early memories and how they are a mixture of recollection and invention. The memory expresses his desire to be completely independent of his father and his family.

For relating these early memories to a parable, he chose Jesus' parable of the wicked tenants. The text of the parable printed in his paper, he says, is "synthesized from Matt. 21:33–38, Luke 20:9–15a, Mark 12:1–8, following primarily the Gospel of Thomas 65:1–8." Here is his version of the text of the parable:[14]

> There was a good man who planted a vineyard, and set a hedge around it, and dug a wine press in it, and built a tower, and let it out to tenants, and went into another country. When the season of fruit drew near, he sent his servant so that the tenants might give him the fruit of the vineyard.

---

14. This amalgamation of different texts is contrary to any accepted critical approach to the passage. I did not object to this treatment of the text, however, and trusted the intuition of the student, unconventional though it was. His early memory takes control of the parable, leaving me with the question, "Did the parable nonetheless do its revelatory work?"

Early Childhood Memories and Jesus' Parables

> They seized his servant and beat him; a little more and they would have killed him. The servant came and told it to his master. His master said, Perhaps they did not know him. He sent another servant; they beat him as well. Then the owner sent his son. He said, Perhaps they will respect my son. Since those tenants knew that he was the heir of the vineyard, they seized him and killed him. Whoever has ears, let them hear.

Jeff explores the views of several interpreters ending up with John Dominic Crossan, who interprets it as a parable of reversal which was the culmination of a larger scheme of reversal in which "normal" stories are juxtaposed with reversal parables to effect a large scale subversion. In it, the bad guys get what they want and the good guys lose. "It is a deliberately shocking story of successful murder." The Kingdom turns perceived reality upside down.[15]

Jeff writes that he does not mention his stepmother in his three early memories although she was part of the family in the second and third recollections. He says he left her out because "I just don't like her."

> I wanted to keep her out of my ERs [early recollections] because I held/hold her responsible for effacing my memories of my mother. Every time I disobeyed my stepmother she carried on about how I only did it because she wasn't really my mother. My guilt-ridden response was repeated so often I came to believe it myself: "But I *do* think of you as my mother, not Judy." This effacement was so thoroughgoing that we [he and his younger brother] were obliged to call our stepmother "mother" and refer to our mother by her first name, "Judy," so as not to offend my stepmother's sensibilities. So as I write this, I am struggling against 20 years of programming designed to have me equate the word "mother" with my stepmother. . . . To see this in writing gives me a strange feeling. I was a primary actor in the story and did not until this writing fully realize the plot. In that sense, I suppose this is part of my myth; it's the fiction in terms of which I've lived my life.

---

15. Crossan, *In Parables*, 94.

Coming back to the parable, I am drawn to Crossan's remark that it relates a story of a successful murder. It definitely describes a situation in which the "good guy" gets his son killed and the murderers are rewarded with the victim's inheritance. I think I see the parable addressing my myth at this point. *My stepmother, with my dad's help, murdered my mother* [student's emphasis]. They didn't push her off a cliff or poison her, but they did almost everything they could to keep her memory from living on in her children. All her personal possessions were given away; if it were not for her parents and her in-laws, my brother and I wouldn't even have a photograph of our mother.

For me, this parable reverses the reversal under which I grew up. My mother, while certainly not perfect, was made out to be the villain. And I would be quite wealthy if I had a nickel for every time my dad tried to get me to understand what a "good mother" my stepmother really was—despite whatever mean and nasty thing she'd just done. Now this story of the vineyard shows that the good aren't necessarily good and the bad can go unpunished. And while Jesus may have told this story, he also said the truth can set one free. And by refusing to participate in the myth, I can be free at least of its direct effects on me.

I am free to incorporate my mother into my story. Like an adopted child who can explain some unique trait as coming from a natural parent, so I can claim my mother's influence in the way I "turned out." I can even claim my life as her legacy, in a manner of speaking. I'm not at all sure what this will mean for my relationship with my parents but in any event I am no longer (as) blind to the situation.

I learned early on that the truth is what you want to believe. No one in our household dared admit there was anything abnormal about my stepmother or her relationship with the family. The suicide attempts/threats, the depressions, the constant illnesses and physical impairments.

Jeff tells that he learned to live in two different realities. One reality was his home and church—his stepmother's father was the pastor—where things revolved around his stepmother's erratic behavior and demands. He saw that outside of home and church, he lived in quite a different reality. He says, "It just didn't make sense to me to be religious outside that environment. In time I did come to sort out the difference between religion and faith but I find the atmosphere at home and at my church to reek of that other reality and as such to be terribly oppressive even today." Then he says,

> The good thing about a parable is its specificity. It doesn't talk about everyone everywhere but about someone somewhere. In that sense, there is only one reality for me: the one in which I live. I have to carry it with me into situations and not allow the situations to impose their reality upon me. My stepmother may be unable to see things any other way but I am not obliged to change my language, personality, memories, and values to humor her. The parable says the son was murdered. The murderers went unpunished, the good guy lost, but the son *was* murdered. The parable can subvert my perception—my myth, it can subvert my stepmother's and my father's myths, but it does not change the reality of what has been done. And so neither does it minimize the challenge involved in my living true to this new perception. With the writing of this I have but just begun and yet already "I stand convicted of impiety / the evidence of my pious duty done."[16]

When I first opened Jeff's paper I was surprised to see a full-page picture of his mother—a beautiful woman who looks to be in her early twenties. He concludes his paper by writing this letter to her:

For My Mother
   I owe you a debt of gratitude I am unable even to express, let alone repay. You gave me life and, what's more, I believe you gave me a love of life. Of the crimes against your memory I can only speak for my own—I deeply regret my culpability. I'm sorry I haven't memories of my own but I'm so grateful for your leaving behind family and friends to

---

16. From Sophocles.

carry that memory for me. Your grandchildren will know you as well as I do, I promise.

I love you and hope to do you proud,
Your son, Jeff

MY CONVERSATION WITH JEFF THIRTY YEARS LATER

As with Alice, I was able to locate Jeff almost thirty years after he wrote this paper. Unlike Alice, he had had the benefit of the small group back then, a community of fellow pilgrims in his class seeking to understand themselves. I asked him what effect this paper had on his life after the course.

He used the analogy of *The Wizard of Oz* and the scene where Dorothy's dog Toto pulls back the curtain to reveal that the great and powerful Oz is only a little man with a grandiose self-presentation. And he added,

> What Dorothy saw behind the curtain wasn't the whole story either. Five or six years later the curtain analogy helped me see my marriage as it really was. Over the next 30 years I periodically recognized things behind the curtain. On my drive home today from work I pulled back the curtain on my job.

He went on to say, "The paper created a psychological distance from my parents that led later to me accepting the relationship we could have. The paper allowed me to make a break. It was like jumping off a diving board. When you jump you can't turn back."

Jeff described the course as "a different kind of academic exercise because it put head and heart together. There was a balance. And I had support from the small group part of the class to experience that balance. Other courses weren't like that. I wish I had kept that balance of head and heart when I did my PhD dissertation."

Finally, he told me, "I remember one evening looking out from a balcony and realizing that the God I had known wasn't there. I would say the class altered my view of God. In fact, it altered my world view.

At that point God and I parted ways. Yet, I continue to feel some connection to what I would call the ineffable."

Alice's interpretation of the parable of the wheat and tares and Jeff's interpretation of the parable of the wicked tenants opened up their early memories to disclose their relationship to family members in a startling light. Rather than producing a lesson or a moral, the parables cracked open long-standing assumptions about their lives, their inner textbook, and subverted their view of reality.

Although the interpretation of these parables by Alice and Jeff may veer off the path of familiar biblical interpretation, clearly they experienced the subversive power of the parables which had the effect of altering their world views. Moreover, they recalled this assignment and its power vividly thirty years later.

MY EARLY MEMORY OF RECITING A RACIST NARRATIVE, AND A PARABLE THAT HAS SUBVERTED IT

As I prepared this chapter, I thought I should take the same risk I asked my students to take—to relate my earliest childhood memories to a parable of Jesus. Here is the result.

My mother loved to perform before an audience. When I was growing up she often did "book reviews," which meant that she told the story of a book—usually a humorous novel. She was quite good at this and usually had some review on her calendar. When I was a child she set about to teach me how to do it. She had me memorize pieces and would find or create occasions for me to perform them. When I was nine or ten, she had me memorize and recite a humorous story about an African American mother and her son "William." I recited this narrative speaking as if I were William's mother. She discovered he had stolen a watermelon. She berated him for this immoral act—going on and on about it. Then she cut the watermelon open and discovered it was not ripe. With this discovery she turned the tables on him and told him how dumb he was not to know the difference between a green and a ripe watermelon.

Jesus' Parable of the Leaven is a counterpoint to my story. "He told them another parable: 'The kingdom of heaven is like yeast that a woman took and mixed in with three measures of flour until all of it was leavened.'"[17]

The apostle Paul sets the stage for my interpretation of this parable. In this translation "leaven" is translated "yeast." He says to the Corinthian church: "Your boasting is not a good thing. Do you not know that a little yeast leavens the whole batch of dough? Clean out the old yeast so that you may be a new batch, as you really are unleavened. . . . Let us celebrate the festival, not with the old yeast, the yeast of malice and evil, but with the unleavened bread of sincerity and truth."[18] Leaven, yeast, was regarded as an unclean substance, which the woman in the parable adds to fifty pounds of flour. What does this mean? Of this parable Bernard Brandon Scott writes,

> The kingdom (the holy and good) is pictured in terms of an epiphany of corruption. How radical is the parable's intention? Does it mean to state that good is evil in an ethics of absurdity? Or is its function to subvert a hearer's ready dependency on the rules of the sacred, the predictability of what is good, and warn that instead the expected evil that corrupts may indeed turn out to be the kingdom.[19]

Blackface: The Distressing History of Minstrel Shows

What I recited in the role of the African American mother has a direct connection to Black minstrels. I played the part of a Black mother—fortunately without the blackened face and a dress. I recall that my mother performed in at least one minstrel show—raising money for our elementary school. What is the origin of the minstrel show?

> Images of black identity created by minstrel shows satirized blacks as singing, dancing, grinning fools. [White] Actors/

---

17. Matt 13:33.
18. 1 Cor 5:6–8.
19. Scott, *Hear Then the Parable*, 328–29.

Early Childhood Memories and Jesus' Parables

musicians blackened their faces with burnt cork and used other make-up material that demeaned African Americans for the pleasure of the viewing audience. . . . Jim Crow is considered to be the first minstrel character, created by Thomas Dartmouth "Daddy" Rice in 1828. Rice was an unemployed actor who said he came upon a black man singing the song "Jump Jim Crow" and imitated that man's mannerisms to construct what became known as the iconic Jim Crow. . . . Within ten years of the character's creation, the term Jim Crow was used as a negative nickname for African Americans . . . By the end of the 19th century Jim Crow was more likely to be used to describe the state laws which limited freedoms and rights of blacks.[20]

How the Parable Challenges My Narrative

The parable's subversive message is that God's dream for humankind is inclusive. And it violates God's dream to claim that one group of people, *our* group, is pure and superior and that another group is impure and inferior. The parable places me and my mother and William and his mother all together as human beings who are loved equally by God. The lines of caste are dissolved in the leaven of the parable. The story of my early memory of performing this piece, a performance that easily belonged to a minstrel show, reveals a part of my Whiteness DNA. I have long ago consciously rejected this kind of racist view. However, as this book attests, I am not free of it.

THE KEYS

Two distinctive types of narrative shaped this chapter—the narrative of parable and the narrative of early childhood memory. These

---

20. This description of the minstrel and Jim Crow comes from Yale University professor Jonathan Holloway's summer teachers' seminar at the Gilder Lehrman Center for the Study of Slavery, Resistance, and Abolition on "The History of Minstrel Shows and Jim Crow," July 2014.

narratives interact with each other to produce an unexpected interpretation of both the early memory and of the parable.

Belonging is a theme in all three of the stories in this chapter. Alice's story opens the chapter with a sibling rivalry between her and her sister about who belongs in her family of origin. Jeff's story tells of the conflict caused by his stepmother who believes she's not accepted as a rightful mother to Jeff and his brother, that she doesn't belong there. His stepmother and his father attempt to exile his birth mother from belonging in the family. The question raised by my story of William and his mother is this: "Do this Black mother and son belong with me and my mother?"

Whiteness and diversity stand out in my story where I, as a White male, portray a Black mother whose inconsistent moral attitude toward theft is an object of ridicule. As a child reciting this story I have the position of a privileged White person looking down on a Black woman—a woman who would represent, in the minds of a minstrel audience, most Black women. The parable subverts my Whiteness. When I put it into dialogue with the story I recited, the parable causes me to see how I have lived in a position of White racial privilege from my childhood to the present. And it is calling me out of that privileged position.

QUESTIONS

1. How have your views on race evolved over your lifetime?
2. What is your earliest childhood memory? What does it tell you about your present life? What happens if you connect it to a parable?
3. If you are a teacher, what might happen if you asked students to tell an early memory of learning such subjects as New Testament, history, ethics, etc.? What might you discover about their personal relationship to you and your course?
4. Does my White recitation of the story of William, his mother, and the theft of a watermelon remind you of a time when you,

as a White person, may have told such a story? If you are a Black person, what is your response to such stories?

5. What do you make of the unorthodox interpretations of the parables in this chapter?

4

Opening Students' Inner Textbooks with Problem-Posing Education

IN THE LAST CHAPTER, you heard two students and me relate our early childhood memories to a parable of Jesus. In our stories, the parables opened up our inner textbooks to disclose important information about which we had little conscious knowledge. How to open students' inner textbooks? These following narratives tell about my relationship to two students and their inner textbooks. (These accounts do not include a parable of Jesus or early memories.)

I follow these narratives with a story of the Brazilian educator Paulo Freire, who learned how to open the inner textbooks of peasants—those who lived at the lowest level of the national economy—as he and his team taught them to read and write.

A STUDENT'S PROBLEM EXPRESSED IN A BAD GRADE

Several years ago, one of my former Southeastern students, whom I shall call Carl, became chair of the deacon council at Pullen Memorial Baptist Church in Raleigh, North Carolina, where we were members. The congregation had been through a crisis, and Carl wrote a letter to the members that was a masterpiece of disclosure, compassion, and wisdom about the crisis and the deacon council's response to it. I wrote him an email to say how much I appreciated what he had written. He wrote me back to thank me for my words. Then he added, "I hope this makes up for the 'D' I got from you in the basic course in pastoral care in 1980." I was startled to see his comment. I didn't remember that I'd given him such a grade.

When I called to ask him about this—some thirty years after the bad grade—I learned that when he took my course he was going through marriage difficulties that finally led to a divorce. He was facing great uncertainty and was doing all he could to keep his head above water. Understandably, his academic work suffered. I gave him a D and was not curious about it. In the basic course in pastoral care my student assistant took care of evaluating tests and keeping track of student grades, I was removed from that process and unaware of Carl's low weekly test scores. He soldiered on bravely through his troubles, not asking for my understanding or help.

His belated account of his experience in my class points directly to the question: "What is effective teaching?" Effective teaching takes into account students' personal stories—including stories disclosed from their inner textbooks. It includes head and heart. Because I made provision in this class for small groups, Carl received support from fellow group members. In fact, he established a life-long friendship with the pastor who facilitated his group. However, my only contact with Carl was his academic performance, and I gave him a bad grade because he was performing poorly. I missed the opportunity to understand the story behind the grade I gave him. I failed in teaching this student.

A STUDENT'S ANGRY PAPER

Several years later I was grading a paper from a man I will call Ronald. What he wrote was an angry criticism of people in the small country church where he was pastor. He wasn't even close to writing about what I had assigned. I started to write a critical response. Then I stopped myself, and I wrote on his paper, "Before I grade your paper I would like to talk with you about it. Would you make an appointment to see me?"

Ronald came to see me, and I told him that I was puzzled by his paper since it did not have anything to do with what had been assigned. Could he help me understand that? He pondered my question and made several false starts. Then he told me he had been having an affair with a woman in his church and this had been going on for some time. Our conversation opened up an opportunity for me to help him decide what to do about this relationship.

Instead of criticizing Ronald about his paper, which was my first inclination, I asked him to help me understand what it meant. To his credit, he had the courage to tell me about this secret emotional and moral predicament that involved a woman in his congregation, his marriage, his family, the congregation itself, and his future in ministry. Although he had no intention of telling me about his affair when he stepped into my office, nonetheless, he was able to respond to my question by opening up his inner textbook to tell the truth about it. It was a redemptive moment for him and for me.

The power of teaching is profoundly diminished when the person of the student is not regarded as an important part of the educational process. In Ronald's case, I was able to discern and respond to a student's moral dilemma. In this he opened his inner textbook to me. For a time, he and I set aside the subject matter of the course to help him deal with his personal moral predicament. In Carl's case, I missed that opportunity.

PAULO FREIRE TEACHING BRAZILIAN PEASANTS TO READ AND WRITE

Here I turn to the work of Paulo Freire, a renowned educator who learned how to open the inner textbooks of the peasants of Brazil as an essential step in teaching them how to read and write. Learning how to educate those who lived in the lowest strata of society led him to develop a revolutionary method of education that he set forth in his book *Pedagogy of the Oppressed*, which, by the time of the fiftieth anniversary of its 1970 English publication in 2020, had sold more than a million copies worldwide. His educational philosophy comes

Opening Students' Inner Textbooks with Problem-Posing Education

through with clarity and power in this book in his understanding of the difference between banking education and problem-posing education. He writes,

> In the banking concept of education, knowledge is a gift bestowed by those who consider themselves knowledgeable upon those whom they consider to know nothing. Projecting an absolute ignorance onto others, a characteristic of the ideology of oppression, negates education and knowledge as processes of inquiry. . . . The *raison d'être* of libertarian education, on the other hand, lies in its drive towards reconciliation. Education must begin with the solution of the teacher-student contradiction, by reconciling the poles of the contradiction so that both are simultaneously teachers *and* students. . . . The capability of banking education to minimize or annul the students' creative power . . . serves the interest of the oppressors, who care neither to have the world revealed nor to see it transformed.[1]

Banking education not only misses opportunities to engage their inner textbooks, it puts students in a passive position, transforming them into receiving objects. It attempts to control thinking and action, inhibiting their creative power. It conditions them to adjust to the world and their place in it rather than to question it, change it, or inform it.[2]

According to Freire, education is always political because it influences the way students relate to their world. Passive students become passive citizens who don't ask critical questions about culture and society. They do not challenge the status quo. For Freire, education isn't really education until it becomes subversive to the status quo, until it leads people to challenge social structures that diminish human wellbeing—particularly the wellbeing of the poor.

Freire's alternative to banking education is problem-posing education in which teacher and students collaborate in the learning process. He writes,

---

1. Freire, *Pedagogy of the Oppressed*, 72–73.
2. Freire, *Pedagogy of the Oppressed*, 77.

> Through dialogue, the teacher-of-the-students and the-students-of-the-teacher cease to exist and a new term emerges: teacher-student with students-teachers. The teacher is no longer merely the-one-who-teaches, but one who is himself [or herself] taught in dialogue with the students, who in turn while being taught also teach. They become jointly responsible for a process in which all grow. In this process, arguments based on "authority" are no longer valid; in order to function authority must be on the side of freedom, not against it. Here no one teaches another, nor is anyone self-taught. People teach each other, mediated by the world, by the cognizable objects which in banking education are "owned" by the teacher.[3]

Instead of receiving blocks of information, the teacher invites students to solve problems—and works with them as they do it. "I engage in dialogue," says Freire, "because I recognize the social and not merely the individualistic character of the process of knowing. In this sense, dialogue presents itself as an indispensable component of the process of both learning and knowing."[4]

Dialogue opens up the inner textbooks of students and their teachers. I opened up a dialogue with Ronald in response to a paper he wrote that failed the assignment completely. Asking him why the assignment didn't fit what was required, I learned that something was wrong, something that went far beyond the assignment, and it desperately needed his teacher's attention. I was able to give him that attention instead of marking his paper with my criticism.

In dialogical teaching, students, in collaboration with those who teach them, seek to discern the nature of what we call "reality." This challenge asks them to uncover the powers that define and defend that "reality." Dialogical teaching encourages students to explore alternative views of "reality" that do not support the status quo.

Ronald's reality was that he had trapped himself in an affair and did not know how to find a way out of it. By writing a paper that had nothing to do with the assignment, he signaled that something was

---

3. Freire, *Pedagogy of the Oppressed*, 80.
4. Freire, *Pedagogy of the Oppressed*, 17.

wrong in his world of reality. Banking education would have left him trapped in the dead end reality of his affair. That reality would have led to a crisis in which everyone involved would suffer without redemption. Ronald and I together were able to discern an alternative reality to the one that had him trapped.

I draw on the work of Paulo Freire because I find that his approach to teaching and learning describes what I have been trying to do during my entire educational career. I discovered Freire when I read William Herzog's *Parables as Subversive Speech: Jesus as Pedagogue of the Oppressed*,[5] in which Herzog compares Jesus' way of teaching parables to first-century Galilean peasants to Freire's way of teaching the peasants of Brazil to read and write. I used Herzog's book in the narrative therapy seminar at Triangle Pastoral Counseling in 2003, where it struck a responsive chord with these professional therapists.

I should add this caveat to my use of Freire. He developed his teaching method working with peasants—the lowest social strata in Brazil. Herzog used Freire's method of working with peasants in Brazil to understand Jesus' method of teaching first-century peasants in Galilee—the lowest social strata in the first century. My teaching method employed the parables of Jesus to do their subversive work on the early recollections of middle-class White students. The parables did remarkable work on these early memories, and the resulting group conversations and the papers which the students wrote testified to the parables' power to open up my students' inner textbooks and mine as well. However, we did not link the parables to the African American experience. We didn't explore that landscape; it did not occur to us to do so.

A Peasant Challenged Freire with a Lesson He Never Forgot

Literacy programs typically taught peasants to read and write using the language of the privileged social classes—those in government, business, social services, religion, etc. Freire's *Pedagogy of the*

---

5. Herzog, *Parables as Subversive Speech*.

Oppressed tells how this privileged language contributed to the peasants' oppression. Those in power devalued and replaced the peasants' language, metaphor, and idiom with their own language of privilege, language that disempowered the peasants. Recognition of this fact came to Freire one evening as he lectured to a large group of peasants giving them reasons, backed by careful research, why they should not use corporal punishment, and at times violent punishment, with their children, but instead should fill their parent-child relationships with dialogue and kindness.

Freire reports that at the end of his lecture, "a man of about forty, still rather young but already worn and exhausted, raised his hand and gave me the clearest and most bruising lesson I have ever received in my life as an educator. . . . It seared my soul for good and all. It has exerted an enormous influence on me. Speaking in a loud, clear voice the man said, 'Dr. Paulo, sir—do you know where people live? Have you ever been in any of our houses, sir?'"

This man described their miserable houses—lack of basic facilities, bodies jammed into small spaces, living on the barest necessities for survival. He spoke of exhaustion and conditions that left them no hope. Then he described what he (accurately) imagined Freire's house to be—a dwelling with adequate space and conveniences. He then proceeded to contrast what Freire's home was like in the evening—children bathed and adequately fed and happy—with *his* home in the evening—children hungry, dirty, noisy, miserable. And he, bone tired, having to get up at four in the morning to go back to work hurting, sad, hopeless. He referred to the main point of Freire's speech about a kinder way to discipline children and said that if his and his neighbors' discipline was harsh, "it's because life is so hard they don't have much choice." Freire was unnerved by this man's eloquent description of their two worlds. As he and his wife Elza drove home, he complained that his audience hadn't understood him. She said, "They understood you, but they needed to have you understand them."

That scene was a turning point in Freire's career as an educator. He realized he could not really teach the peasants without

Opening Students' Inner Textbooks with Problem-Posing Education

participating in their lives.[6] By the end of his life, Freire had received numerous honors as an educator. But he always remembered that one incident with the peasant man. "In almost every academic ceremony in which I am honored," he said, "I see him standing in one of the aisles of that big auditorium of so long ago, head erect, eyes blazing, speaking in a loud, clear voice, sure of himself, speaking his lucid speech."[7]

The above encounter and others like it led Freire to conduct his literacy program by first learning how the peasants thought and communicated with each other. He established interdisciplinary teams to join him *in living with peasants in order to understand their view of the world*—their language, metaphors, and sense of despair and hopelessness.

As they participated in the life of the peasants, Freire and his teams had this challenge: How could they who enjoyed the privileges of the upper class strata of society understand the peasants who lived far from such privilege? Freire saw that he could not understand the world of the peasants until he allowed them to teach him what their life was like. This was not easy for him or for his teams. How could they participate in groups of peasants and not draw on their accustomed, privileged way of seeing things? As they allowed the peasants to teach them about their life and their world view, Freire and his teams saw how the peasants had internalized the world of their oppressors so that they looked upon themselves the way the elite did—as deserving their miserable way of life. They lived in the social construction of reality of the aristocracy. They had been the object of "banking education" that "aimed at depositing the worldview of the dominant class in the peasants' minds and hearts, thereby persuading them that they were nothing more than objects in the reality of the ruling elites."[8]

As he allowed the peasants to teach him and his teams about their lives, Freire and his teams began to see the rich values, practices,

---

6. Freire, *Pedagogy of Hope*, 18–27.
7. Freire, *Pedagogy of Hope*, 24.
8. Herzog, *Parables as Subversive Speech*, 19.

and relationships of peasant society. And they then were able to use these values, practices, and relationships as resources in teaching the peasants to read and write in language that reflected their own cherished traditions and not the traditions of the privileged classes.

Because they had "banked" or internalized the elite view of them, the peasants did not value their own tradition, their own way of looking at the world, of relating to each other, of facing their life's incredible difficulties.

I believe I pursued an educational practice that aimed toward Freire's understanding of it. I translate Freire for my work as a teacher this way.

Banking education delivers content that students are expected to take in, then demonstrate their knowledge of by taking tests, responding in class, and writing papers. The content usually supports conventional wisdom, and therefore students are most often educated to serve established power structures and to do so uncritically.

In *problem-posing education* students do not receive "settled truth" from their teachers but rather, in collaboration with teachers, they are challenged to solve problems. Through critical analysis of the problem, they develop their own understanding of the content they must explore in order to solve the problem.

In this process students are drawn into using their personal resources—their own history and the history of their family and its traditions. They draw deeply on what lies inside their inner textbooks.

And in this problem-posing education students learn to penetrate what those in power say is "reality" to discover alternative views of "reality." These alternative views liberate them to see their lives and their world differently than they appear in the conventional wisdom of society.

PAULO FREIRE AND THE PARABLES OF JESUS

In 1994, William Herzog, then vice president for academic life, dean of the faculty, and professor of New Testament interpretation at Colgate Rochester Divinity School, published the aforementioned

Opening Students' Inner Textbooks with Problem-Posing Education

Parables as Subversive Speech: Jesus as Pedagogue of the Oppressed. Herzog saw in Freire's *Pedagogy of the Oppressed* a parallel to the way Jesus used parables to help first-century peasants interpret their world of oppression. Herzog's interpretation of the Parable of the Talents is a case in point.

> For it is as if a man, going on a journey, summoned his slaves and entrusted his property to them; to one he gave five talents, to another two, to another one, to each according to his ability. Then he went away. The one who had received the five talents went off at once and traded with them, and made five more talents. In the same way, the one who had the two talents made two more talents. But the one who had received the one talent went off and dug a hole in the ground and hid his master's money.

When the master returned, he demanded a reckoning and praised the first and second servants for doubling his money. The third servant tells the master: "Master, I knew that you were a harsh man, reaping where you did not sow, and gathering where you did not scatter seed; so I was afraid, and I went and hid your talent in the ground. Here you have what is yours."[9]

The master condemned the third servant for burying what he'd received instead of doubling his money the way the other two servants have done. Matthew understands this story as a parable of the last judgment and has added this: "As for this useless servant, throw him out into the dark, where there will be wailing and grinding of teeth!"

Ernesto Cardenal, a priest in Solentiname, Nicaragua, taught this same parable to a group of twentieth-century peasants, and he reports how the peasants refused to accept Matthew's interpretation of the story in which the master condemned the third servant. They said that the parable was "a very ugly example of exploitation, of speculation with money." One of them, Oscar, said the master "looked for others who were exploiters like him" to double his money by taking advantage of "the people." These peasants saw clearly how

---

9. The text of the parable is Matt 25:14–27; verses 28–30 are a later addition.

the first two servants made a 100 percent profit the only way they could—by exploiting the peasants who worked on the estate—for example, loaning them money when they had a bad crop year, charging them exorbitant interest, and then foreclosing on their land when they couldn't pay. The Solentiname peasants saw the third servant as the hero of the parable because he refused to take advantage of the peasants in order to double the master's money—and because he unmasked the overwhelming greed and ruthlessness of the master.

Herzog writes that "of all the contemporary commentators on the parable, the peasants of Solentiname were the ones to intuit the economic system that underlies the parable." The peasants "got it" whereas most of the scholars didn't. In the parable, Jesus challenges his peasant audience to take a careful look at their situation and how their master and others like him have condemned them to live in fear and desperation.[10] The parable discloses that the way they are living is not God's dream for them.[11] Jesus reveals that God's dream subverts their belief in the master's view of them, and he gives them an entirely different narrative of their worth in God's eyes.

The work of Freire and Herzog sheds light on the teaching method I had been developing during my career as a seminary professor. It provides a theoretical and theological frame of reference that supports my teaching strategy of pairing early childhood memory with a parable of Jesus. In this strategy I presented the students with a problem to be solved—one that had the potential to subvert their familiar way of seeing themselves and their world.

THE REALITY OF RACE AND CASTE

Now this educational perspective requires a further renovation as I deal with the reality of race and caste—that thick, neglected layer of culture and history that my study of Whiteness now unfolds before me.

---

10. Herzog, *Parables as Subversive Speech*, 155–61.
11. Tutu, *God Has a Dream*.

Opening Students' Inner Textbooks with Problem-Posing Education

When I was a college student at Baylor University from 1957 to 1961, I learned a lesson from William Toland, professor of philosophy, that profoundly influenced my way of understanding the world. It was the most important thing I learned in my college education, and yet it was a lesson so countercultural that I had to keep relearning it. The course was "The Philosophy of History." In that course I learned that historians have biases, whether they admit them or not. And that any historical account is told from the particular angle of the historian. Out of the welter of data of a historical period, historians select those facts that conform to their worldview and leave other facts aside, creating an unavoidably biased account. For my presentation in this class, I chose Nicolas de Condorcet (1743–94), a French philosopher, mathematician, and political scientist. In this assignment, I showed how Condorcet, in his *Sketch for a Historical Picture of the Progress of the Human Mind*,[12] selected historical material to confirm his belief in human progress and ignored evidence to the contrary. Working on the Condorcet problem-posing assignment opened my eyes to recognize that there is no such thing as objective history. This discovery led me eventually to understand that we don't have direct access to reality, only biased reports of it.

The manuscript of this book is an example of such bias. In these accounts of my teaching experience I have gathered information that was apparent and readily accessible to me. I did not, however, investigate a history that was largely hidden from me for most of my life—the history of slavery and systemic racism in America. As I now revise this manuscript, it is clear to me that this understanding of biased history is a light that we urgently need to shine on the suppressed accounts of the horrors of slavery and racial oppression that are deeply woven into the fabric of American history. Nowhere

---

12. Marie-Jean-Antoine-Nicolas de Caritat, Marquis de Condorcet (1743–94), was a French philosopher of the Enlightenment who was a principal figure in formulating the idea of historical progress—the belief that humankind is moving inexorably toward a state of perfection. While in hiding during the French Revolution in 1794, he wrote *Sketch for a Historical Picture of the Progress of the Human Mind*, which was published in 1795.

is this suppression of America's racist history more striking than in American history as it has been taught in our public schools.

Donald Yacovone, an associate at the Hutchins Center for African and African American Research at Harvard University, investigated Harvard's Gutman Library collection of nearly three thousand US history school textbooks, dating from about 1800 to the 1980s. He wanted to know "how abolitionism, race, slavery, and the Civil War and Reconstruction have been taught in our nation's school books from the 1830s to the present." This is his assessment:

> The assumptions of white priority and white domination suffuse every chapter and every theme of the thousands of textbooks that have blanketed the schools of our country. This vast tectonic plate *still* underlies American culture and we ignore it at our peril. While the worst features of our textbook legacy have ended, as the recently published study (2018) by the Southern Poverty Law Center, *Teaching Hard History: American Slavery* shows, our schools are still ignoring the difficult issues raised by our past, and the themes, facts, and attitudes of supremacist ideologies remain embedded in our national identity, in what we teach, and in what we learn.... Historians of the twentieth century exerted an *enormous* impact on the way modern Americans have come to understand their history.... To appreciate why white supremacy remains such an integral part of current American society, we need to appreciate how much it suffused our teaching from the outset.[13]

"If America is to be a nation that fulfills its democratic promise," Yacovone says, "the history of slavery and white supremacy have to be taught in schools across the country. We need to acknowledge that white supremacy remains an integral part of American society and we need to understand how we got to where we are.... White supremacy is a toxin." And many of the textbooks Yacovone investigated, he says, "were like syringes that injected the toxin of white supremacy into the mind of many generations of Americans. What

---

13. Yacovone, "Teaching White Supremacy."

has to be done is teach the truth about slavery as a central institution in America's origins."[14]

Yacovone continued his investigation of the teaching about race in US education, and in September 2022 he published *Teaching White Supremacy: America's Democratic Ordeal and the Forging of Our National Identity*. In this book he says that despite the publication of textbooks that give thorough and accurate accounts of slavery and the oppression of people of color, and despite the abundance of such historical information on the internet, the teaching of the history of slavery, the Civil War, and the ongoing oppression of people of color is woefully inadequate. Accurate historical reports of Black history and the effects of White privilege have met angry opposition. The American Textbook Council, established in 1989, "waged total war on advocates of new history school curriculum." The Council's director, Gilbert T. Sewall, said that the trend toward multiculturalism had swung so far to the left that it crowded out "the old master narratives" of "faith in progress and patriotic pride." History, he claimed, had been reduced to condemnations of a nation that had fallen short of its ideals.

Yacovone cites other forces that have made it difficult to teach history that is faithful to the actual events of the past rather than extolling an unrealized ideal. Private schools have provided a haven to protect students from the racist history of this country. For example, as of 2020 175,680 school age White children lived in the city of Chicago, but only 37,198 attended public schools, representing 10.9 percent of the public school population. Adding to these problems is the fact that the teaching of history has been neglected in public school curricula at every level. And that responsibility has often been given to teachers with only minimal background or preparation to teach it.[15]

If I were teaching now, I would take up two tasks. The first would be to teach White and Black students together. If I were still teaching at Southeastern Baptist Theological Seminary in Wake Forest, North

---

14. Yacovone, "How Textbooks Taught."
15. Yacovone, *Teaching White Supremacy*, 309–27.

Carolina, and if the majority of students were still White, I would seek some kind of cooperative effort with the faculty of nearby Shaw University Divinity School in which that school's African American students and my White students could learn together. The second task I would take up would be to make it part of my teaching responsibility, whatever subject I was teaching, to include the story of race and caste in America. This book, in fact, shows how that can be done.

PATRIARCHY, THE TAP ROOT OF CASTE AND RACIAL INEQUALITY

I have come to see that patriarchy and the subordination of women underlies all caste and racial issues. This view is supported by critical studies of Jesus' view of the family. Walter Wink writes that

> the family was the most basic instrument of nurture, social control, enculturation, and training in Jewish society. . . . Yet Jesus, consistent with his critique of domination, had almost nothing good to say about families. "Whoever comes to me and does not hate father and mother, wife and children, brothers and sisters, yes, and even life itself, cannot be my disciple." . . . Why is he so extreme? . . . I believe Jesus was so consistently disparaging because the family in dominator societies is so deeply embedded in patriarchy, and serves as the citadel of male supremacy, the chief inculcator of gender roles, and a major inhibitor of change.[16]

In the next chapter I will explore further Jesus' view of the first-century patriarchal family and his creation of a new non-patriarchal one. At this point I want to discuss something much closer to my personal life—how my wife and I have dealt with patriarchy in our family.

---

16. Wink, *Powers That Be*, 75–76.

Opening Students' Inner Textbooks with Problem-Posing Education

PATRIARCHY, RACE, AND GENDER BIAS IN MY MARRIAGE

Upon graduation from Baylor University in 1961, freshly married to Beverly Raney, we set out for Louisville, Kentucky, and I enrolled at the Southern Baptist Theological Seminary where I pursued my BD and PhD degrees. To support us, Beverly took a job as a social worker at the Jefferson County Welfare Department. Since college, when she had taken a course from sociologist Charles Wilson, she had intended to pursue a professional career in social work. That dream, however, had been put on hold when we got married. As we arrived in Louisville for me to pursue my professional education, neither of us considered the possibility of her getting an MSW from the University of Louisville Kent School of Social Work—located just a few miles from the seminary—while I was getting my theological degree.

Although her desire was to become a master's level social worker, neither of us had a plan for how this would happen. In the next few years we moved to two different locations because of my employment. In neither location was it possible for her to begin graduate studies at a school of social work. However, while I was teaching at Phillips Theological Seminary in Enid, Oklahoma, during the 1970s, she began to take courses there that led to completion of a master's degree in guidance and counseling—a step toward her goal. After our move to North Carolina, she was finally able to complete the master of social work degree for which she had waited nineteen years, graduating from the University of North Carolina at Chapel Hill in May 1982. She soon secured her credential as a licensed clinical social worker. This gradual process took years and involved a sea change in our thinking about gender equality. I had to let go of my biased, paternalistic world view—or at least loosen my grip on it—and she had to claim her rightful place of equality.

Beverly was the primary person who taught me to confront my patriarchal outlook. Other women also taught me, including our daughter Ann, female colleagues, and students. Learning how to change my patriarchal outlook is an ongoing task. A few days before writing this paragraph, Beverly and I were having lunch with a woman in her eighties who had led a company that manufactured and installed industrial air conditioning. I asked her, "How long did you lead the company after your husband died?" She said, "He never had anything to do with it. It was my company from the beginning."

African American womanist theologian Clarice Martin, Jean Picker Professor of Philosophy and Religion at Colgate University, describes how paternalism distorted history in order to subordinate women and to minimize the plight of slaves. She says, "Womanist biblical interpreters . . . must engage in a multipronged investigative analysis and critique of the tendencies of the biblical writers and traditioning process." Texts in that traditioning process, she says, "convey little information about the agency of slaves and manumission of slaves in the early Christian movement because these stories, like the stories of women, were considered to be either insignificant or a threat to the gradual patriarchalization of the Christian movement."[17]

If you pursue the issue of female-male equality, you have to deal with paternalism, and when you attempt to understand paternalism, you will encounter the world view of Whiteness. Paternalism certainly occurs in all racial groups, but White paternalism reigns over it all.

RACIAL AND GENDER BIAS IN MY GRADUATE WORK

For my graduate research and dissertation under the supervision of Wayne Oates, I designed a research project with seventeen theological students who were enrolled in clinical pastoral education in a cluster of teaching hospitals in Louisville, Kentucky. My research took place in 1965 and 1966. The Civil Rights Act of 1964 had preceded my research by only a few months. Of these hospitals, Louisville General Hospital and Children's Hospital were charity hospitals that historically had served African Americans.

My thesis title was "Attitudes Toward Pastoral Authority Among Selected Theological Students." Data for my research came from the

---

17. Martin, "Womanist Interpretations," 39.

students' religious autobiographies, my taped interviews with them, their testing by a clinical psychologist, and supervisors' evaluations of them. Continuing my nascent understanding of the bias in any historical account, I wrote a long section about bias in clinical research, and I gave examples from my research with these seminarians. One bias that stood out among others was the fact that my subjects were young novices in ministry. Pastoral authority was an idea remote from their experience. It was too much to expect them to understand how they might express pastoral authority. I was asking a question they weren't ready to answer.

But what about gender and racial attitudes? I was doing research with an all-male and all-White group. I was not listening for feminine (let alone feminist) voices. Franz Boas, pioneering anthropologist at Columbia University in the first half of the twentieth century, worked to bring more women into the graduate program. He believed that a science that had access to only half of the available data—the practices, stories, and rituals of men—was no science at all.[18] The absence of ethnic diversity in my research was a second deficiency and a serious one. James Baldwin says the color line corrupts or compromises all American efforts to build a better world.[19] In my research and thesis I allowed the color line to restrict my research subjects to an all white group just as I restricted it to an all male group. I failed here on both counts to be inclusive.

The students were chaplains to African Americans and other people of color, and they regularly interacted with doctors, nurses, and other staff who were not White. In their two semesters of clinical pastoral education, they spent long hours in hospitals where they had repeated contact with people of color. Moreover, they were interacting with women every day. Of all the questions I asked, I did not ask them about their racial or gender attitudes or how they experienced providing pastoral care to women and to persons of color.

Despite these issues that now are so clear to me—issues my graduate supervisor and committee did not raise—Wayne Oates was

18. King, *Gods of the Upper Air*, 118.
19. Baldwin, *Fire Next Time*, 103.

an excellent graduate supervisor. I would turn in a chapter for his review one day and get it back the next. He supported my ideas and tested them with helpful questions, but he never tried to impose his ideas on me. He supported me to be on my own journey. It was never his journey. This was a powerful demonstration of problem-posing education.

THE KEYS

Two *student narratives* frame this chapter—Carl's story of getting a D in my class years ago, and Ronald's story of having an affair with a woman in his church. I didn't recognize that Carl's marital crisis accounted for his low grade, but I did recognize that Ronald's off-target, angry term paper was a clue that he was struggling with a problem. The *primary narrative* in the chapter is the story of Paulo Freire's method of teaching literacy to the peasants of Brazil and how William Herzog used Freire's educational approach to interpret Jesus' parables.

Belonging. I identified patriarchy as the tap root of systemic oppression and noted that Jesus rejected his biological family's claims on him. Patriarchy requires *all who want to belong* to pay the price of submission to patriarchal control. Jesus resisted patriarchal control and taught parables that sought to liberate peasants from the patriarchal control of their masters. Paulo Freire discovered that to teach the peasants of Brazil he had to dismantle established paternalistic educational structures.

Diversity and Whiteness. The biased condition of US history textbooks is stunning. These textbooks protect a story of White superiority and conceal a story of the White exploitation and abuse of people of color. They do not tell the story of 250 years of slavery in this country and the subsequent century and a half of systemic racial oppression. In these textbooks diversity is rejected in order to tell a lie about this country's history. As I did research and wrote my doctoral thesis I was unaware of the biases created by the lack of diversity in the group I was studying—all male and all White, not to mention all middle class.

QUESTIONS

1. How have you experienced the tension between banking education and problem-posing education? What examples do you have of these contrasting types of education?
2. What is a story about something you learned in your educational journey that's stayed with you for ten or twenty years or more? Why do you think it stuck in your mind?
3. What story do you have of being an advocate of racial justice?
4. What has been your experience of learning about the history of slavery and racial oppression since the first slaves arrived in Virginia in 1619?
5. What has been your experience with the power of paternalism?

5

Families: Where Theology Begins

GROWING UP IN SEGREGATED Ft. Worth, Texas, I knew one Black man. His name was Ben Cole. From time to time, my parents hired him to do yard work for us. I recall our family visiting acquaintances where Ben lived. He had a small house behind their house, and, in exchange for rent, he tended their yard. I had never seen such a lush and beautiful yard before, and I stared at it in wonder. Ben had created a luxurious paradise of plants.

I enjoyed being around Ben when he was working in our yard. I was about nine years old and talking with him. He told me something that I didn't understand, and I said, "Sir?" to get him to repeat it. When I next went into the house, Mother told me, "We don't say 'sir' to Negroes." I did not question her. That admonition was a negative counterweight to the knowledge I had of Ben's exceptional ability to create beauty.

Both of my parents grew up in Goldthwaite, Texas, where I often visited both sets of my grandparents. Goldthwaite was all White, and as a child I learned that "colored people aren't allowed to stay in Goldthwaite after dark." I accepted this information without question. Goldthwaite was a "sundown town" along with as many as ten thousand others across the country. Racial prohibition in these towns occurred during the Great Migration, starting about 1910, when large numbers of African Americans moved out of the South

Families: Where Theology Begins

to escape poverty and racism. Sundown towns took overt or covert measures to keep Black people from settling there—prohibiting them from even lingering after dark.[1]

This sundown prohibition in Goldthwaite possibly lasted well into the 1980s as indicated by a story told by an African American student from Howard Payne University in Brownwood, Texas, who had a tire go flat as he was driving through Goldthwaite on his way to Brownwood. He didn't stop to change the tire. He kept on driving on the flat because he had been told that the town used to have a sign at the city limits that said something like "No Negroes after Sundown."[2]

My Whiteness covered over these facts of racial discrimination, intimidation, and oppression—facts that lay undisturbed in my mind until they were brought to the surface by the events of "Black Lives Matter" and my study of Whiteness informed by Benjamin Boswell's Whiteness project. I felt liberated by the discovery of my Whiteness and the revision of my world view it has required; however, this is a work in progress.

In this chapter I tell how in a course on family process I introduced the idea that we carry with us two sets of beliefs—our formal beliefs which we consciously think about and express and our functional beliefs that exist mostly outside of our awareness. Our functional beliefs often override our formal beliefs.

The idea of formal and functional beliefs is a variant expression of the idea of the conscious and unconscious dimensions of our thought and emotion first described by Sigmund Freud. Using the term *belief* locates the idea within the realm of religion and theology, and that was the focus in this class. What are the formal and functional beliefs in our families of origin?

I have told the story of my experience as pastor of Parkview Baptist Church in Gainesville, Florida, and how I became involved in the Black community. However, as I confessed in that chapter, I did not deal with my Whiteness in that experience. That is, I did not

---

1. Coen, "Sundown Towns."

2. Loewen, "Goldthwaite." For a more complete account of sundown towns in America see Loewen, *Sundown Towns*.

reckon with the power I carried as a White person in a multi-racial world. I did not comprehend the remarkable privileges I had by being White. And I still have trouble recognizing and acknowledging these privileges.

All of my life I have lived on one side of a street called race, and people of color have lived on the other side. This street is like an interstate highway that slices through neighborhoods cutting off the severed parts from each other. Yes, I knew there was a Black world over there. But with the exception of my two and a half years as pastor of Parkview Baptist Church, I seldom went over to the other side of that street. My wife did go over to the other side. Soon after our arrival in Louisville, Kentucky, where I would go to seminary, Beverly got a job at the Jefferson County Welfare Department where she worked with a fully integrated multi-racial staff. There she not only did her work, she made Black friends, and one of those colleagues became a life-long friend. As a clinical social worker all of her jobs have been in integrated staffs that provided services to multi-racial populations.

How has racial prejudice been at work in my virtually all-White existence? No White person in America can live without having four hundred years of racial oppression and White privilege indelibly imprinted on his or her conscience. The awakening to my Whiteness that I have so far described, and that has deepened with the re-writing of this book, has taken me to explore the other side of this racial street.

As I have gone over to the other side of this racial interstate highway I have recognized prejudices that express my functional theology. Recently I saw a man riding on the most beautiful red motorcycle I had ever seen. It was a brand new Harley-Davidson. I was enjoying this vision when the rider stopped and took off his helmet, and I saw that the was Black. Here, in a split second, my functional theology kicked in and I thought, "No, the rider of such a splendid motorcycle couldn't be Black." I quickly censored that thought, telling myself, "It's perfectly all right for the rider to be Black, that's my racism talking." This event does not seem remarkable; i.e., for me to have this double-take on race. And it isn't singular. It happens frequently. I work against it, but it is there to remind me again and again of my racism.

My formal theology declares, "All races are equal, and your Whiteness does not entitle you to special privileges reserved for White people." My functional theology tells me, "You see people of color as second class human beings, and you observe this often." With this perspective on the difference between formal belief and functional belief, I turn to the story of a student who struggled to untangle these two belief patterns in the family she grew up in.

DEIFICATION OF A PARENT

Angela is single, in her mid-twenties, and the eldest of two daughters. She narrates her earliest childhood recollection:

> When I was about five years old my mother came as she usually did to pick up my little three-year-old sister and me at our nursery. My sister and I were especially excited that day because our babysitter had given us both an armful of her old pocketbooks to play with and we were going to get to take them home.
>
> On the way home my car door came open and I fell out on the main highway and busted my head open. My mother, without realizing what had happened, continued to drive a few feet. I thought she was leaving me. After realizing what had happened she stopped the car and in somewhat [of] a state of shock sent my little sister back to see if I was all right. My sister, not really knowing what to do, came to me and just picked up the pocketbooks I was carrying and ran back to the car. By this time my mother was running out to me in the middle of the street where I lay bleeding. She picked me up and put me in the car and we stopped by my father's office to get him and they carried me to the hospital.
>
> My story really begins with my parents before I was born. My mother was the next to the youngest in a family of twelve. . . . My daddy was the oldest of three. . . . He was seven years older than Mama and was her high school

teacher. They became engaged Mama's senior year in high school. But two months before her graduation she found out she was pregnant, so she and Daddy were married in June. Seven months later I was born.

Angela wrote this paper for the class "Theology and Self-Understanding," as did Alice and Jeff, whose narratives appeared in chapter 2. You'll recall that the assignment in Alice's and Jeff's class was to relate their early childhood memory to a parable of Jesus. Angela had taken an earlier class in which the assignment was more open—to relate her earliest childhood memory to one or more biblical narratives.

Here I reiterate that although our functional beliefs for the most part reside outside our conscious awareness, they exert a powerful influence—more often than not outweighing the influence of our formal beliefs.

Angela continues her story by describing her mother's criticism of her and her sense that she wasn't good enough:

> All through my childhood I remember feeling that Mama was mad at me for something and that I just didn't measure up. So I tried so hard to make her love me. . . . I thought that if I just did the right things then maybe she would love me more. But I was a clumsy child—the one who broke everything. I was the one who always got sick. I was the one who always lost things. I was the one who only made C's. Yet, the harder I tried to "be good," the bigger mess I made of things.
>
> All of this is so hard to write because my mind is racing so fast that I can hardly get it all in. For although it is true, and now I can see it in retrospect, that deep down I did not feel that Mama loved me, as a child I would never let myself think that thought. Whenever I would feel sad and think that Mama didn't love me, I would make myself stop and I would say, "That's not nice to think things like that about your mama—you are bad for thinking that—of course your mama loves you."

Angela said that before this class she could have spoken about what she'd written to this point, but she could not have expressed the emotion that comes out in this paper. She could do this only after she had gone to the seminary chaplain to talk about the pain she felt. With the chaplain's help she was able to acknowledge and express her feelings of rejection—"feelings [that] up to this time I would not even let myself feel, let alone tell them to anybody else."

With this family history, she approached the Bible to find narratives that would connect with her story, as her class assignment required. She selected three: Abraham sacrificing Isaac (Gen 22:1-19), Nicodemus hearing from Jesus, "You must be born again" (John 3:1-4), and the rich young ruler whom Jesus told, "Go, sell your possessions, and give the money to the poor . . . then come follow me" (Matt 19:16-22). She read these texts through the lens of the functional beliefs she had acquired in her family. She says,

> I felt like Isaac all my childhood. I had to be sacrificed all my life for something I had nothing to do with. I was just born and for that fact I had to suffer. Unlike when she picked me up in the road and Abraham took Isaac down from the altar, I realize I cannot just lie there hurting, afraid, not feeling accepted, and wait for Mama to change. If I am going to be free from this sacrificing altar, I must gather enough energy—no matter how badly it hurts—and take myself off the altar.

From this astonishing interpretation, she turned to the other two texts.

> At times I felt like Nicodemus—confused and astounded at what I perceived being told me by the one I respected the most and the one by whom I most wanted to be accepted. "You must be born again." How in the world can I start all over? I am here and there is nothing I can do about it.
>
> I felt like the Rich Young Ruler who did everything in his power to be accepted. All his actions and his desires seemed to be genuine. Then he was told to give up his riches. Give up everything you have. My mother wants that of me—my life—for in a way I took hers away simply by being born. Now it's as if I owe her all I have and all I am to make up for the fact that "I am." Like the Young Ruler, I have decided that I will have to walk away from my mother.

After she'd written her first interpretations of these texts, Angela took a second look at them and described how she viewed these first interpretations as misreadings of the texts.

> I see how this is a distorted view of the scriptural story. For God did not leave Isaac there to struggle alone to free himself. God gave the lamb [actually a ram]. I think God is telling me also that he/she does not want me to struggle alone, but that the Almighty has given me a community around me to help in this process. God this semester has allowed me to share in my group and through my papers so that it hasn't been me just trying to come up with the energy all within myself. Yet the greatest thing God has provided is the lamb—Jesus Christ who has come to set the captive free. This is not only good news to me, but to Mama as well. No longer does she have to live out her guilt and frustration through me. Jesus offers us both new life. We are both persons of worth and value, for we are daughters of God. I'm glad I've seen that and I hope one day Mama will.

She continued this work with her other two narratives—Jesus and Nicodemus and Jesus and the rich young ruler.

> In these last two scripture stories I have equated my mother with Jesus. That has been my whole problem. I indeed must be born again and must give up all I have, but not to my mother—to Jesus Christ. She is not the final authority in my life and until now I have been confusing the will of mama [with] the will of God, the Mother/Father of all. I can rest assured that I can give my all to the Almighty with no fear of abandonment or [of] not being accepted. My worth comes as a child of the living most high God. That's grounds for celebration!

Angela says her first interpretations of these three texts were misreadings. I think these texts, as she first interpreted them, opened up her inner textbook in a remarkable way. There she found the honest truth about herself and her mother that, up to now, she had refused to believe. Should we call it a misreading when biblical texts penetrate to one's very soul as these accounts seemed to do with her?

At the end of her paper she told that she'd been home for the weekend and was able to look more honestly at her mother. "I went away feeling more secure and more loved than I ever had before, when I was trying to live up to some kind of standard. I love my mama and I am glad that now I can see her as a human, a fellow struggler rather than a god."

A FAMILY'S FORMAL BELIEFS VS. ITS FUNCTIONAL BELIEFS

In any educational process, learning occurs as students relate the beliefs they've brought with them into the classroom with the knowledge being taught. I describe this as working with formal beliefs—those that are conscious and available for exploration. Beneath these formal beliefs lie functional beliefs—those that are unconscious and not immediately available for exploration. Angela's functional belief emerged from her mother's out-of-wedlock pregnancy with her high school teacher for which her mother feels God's judgment. Angela, the child of the pregnancy, is a constant reminder of that judgment. This leads her mother to treat Angela as an unwanted intruder. That disruption in the mother-daughter relationship led Angela to organize her life around winning her mother's love. That's her functional belief—a belief that resides in her inner textbook—something she couldn't consciously admit to herself until her work in this class.

Narrative therapists Alan Perry and Robert Doan reflect on the work of Sigmund Freud in a way that describes the tension between formal and functional beliefs. They write that Freud developed his theory of therapy by listening to patients' stories. He invited them to tell whatever they needed to tell, letting the words flow freely. As the patients talked, sooner or later they would stumble over unaccountable gaps in their stories.

> Those gaps would be filled by forgotten experiences, which often were at shocking variance with the versions that had been put in the individuals' mouths by others. Suddenly their own versions of lost experiences enabled them to find

their own voices to describe their own experiences. Their lives began to make sense, and they had stories of their own; they were no longer compelled to live as supporting characters in stories that had gone forward at their expense.

Freud found that his patients were carrying around and using other people's words—primarily those of their parents, as well as the strictures of society—to describe their experiences. Beneath these conscious stories Freud elicited unconscious narratives in which his patients discovered their own voices, their own words, their own stories.[3]

Early childhood memories have a revelatory power similar to Freud's discovery that patients would fill "gaps" in the free flow of their narrative with their versions of "lost experiences" in their families of origin. These early memories, when laid beside a provocative text—such as Angela's choice of Abraham sacrificing Isaac—revealed that they had been "carrying around and using other people's words" rather than their own. Angela's story and the stories of Alice and Jeff in the earlier chapter are accounts of them discovering their own voice. The stories of these three students reveal the creative power of the unconscious—a dimension of their inner textbooks. As they became aware of what's hidden in their unconscious, they had a choice: they could continue to be supporting characters in stories that had gone forward at their expense, or they could write their own stories.

On her way to finding her own voice, Angela "misinterpreted" the story of Abraham intending to sacrifice Isaac—known in Judaism as the "Akedah" or "binding." It turns out that her interpretation is very close to an interpretation by Alice Miller, a Swiss psychoanalyst who studied thirty artists' portrayals of this story of Abraham and Isaac. Miller says, "In all the portrayals of this scene that I found, Abraham's face or entire torso is turned away from his son and directed upward. Only his hands are occupied with the sacrifice." She says further, "The son, an adult at the peak of his manhood, is simply lying there, quietly waiting to be murdered by his father. . . . In none of the paintings can we detect any questioning in Isaac's eyes, such

---

3. Doan and Parry, *Story Re-Visions*, 8.

as, 'Father, why do you want to kill me, why is my life worth nothing to you? . . . I love you, I trusted in you. Why won't you speak to me. What crime have I committed? What have I done to deserve this.'"[4] Angela's remarkable interpretation deserves to be repeated here. In this case functional belief won out over her formal belief about biblical narratives.

> Unlike when she picked me up in the road and Abraham took Isaac down from the altar, I realize I cannot just lie there hurting, afraid, not feeling accepted, and wait for Mama to change. If I am going to be free from this sacrificing altar, I must gather enough energy—no matter how badly it hurts—and take myself off the altar.

AN ENCOUNTER WITH MY MOTHER REVEALS MY FORMAL AND FUNCTIONAL BELIEF

When I was in my early twenties and a second-year theological student, my mother came to visit us. She'd been there a few days when my wife of less than two years expressed tearful dismay because my mother had taken over the kitchen and was preparing all our meals. Beverly felt displaced. I told Mother that although she was being helpful, she needed to stay out of the kitchen. This event tapped into years of unacknowledged and unexpressed anger I had toward her. My response about the kitchen, and about other things she was doing during that visit that annoyed me, so distressed her that she did not speak to me for at least a year.

Mother and I were enacting a drama in which from early childhood I had treated her as a deity who must not be challenged. I was afraid of her anger and did my best to avoid setting it off. She had a similar relationship with her own mother. On this occasion, however, by my words and actions I finally was saying, "No, you aren't god to me." Unfortunately, I didn't handle my theological awakening with kindness toward her. She never expected such a response from

---

4. Miller, *Untouched Key*, 138.

me, and she felt totally rejected. Mother and I eventually became reconciled when Beverly and I had our first child.

This event was a critical point in my theological education because it awakened me to the unconscious functional belief I'd been living with most of my life. I should add that I filled her place as a god with other authority figures as I continued to experience the tension between my formal and functional beliefs. Before long, Wayne Oates, the professor that supervised my graduate work, took her place in my mind as a deity.

DOING DESCRIPTIVE THEOLOGICAL WORK ON ONE'S FAMILY

In our course on families, my colleague Furman Hewitt and I asked students to write about their family of origin over three generations—themselves, their parents, and their grandparents, or parental figures who filled these roles. We had them study the Bowen Family Systems understanding of the multigenerational process in families.[5] And we introduced them to the idea that they carry with them two sets of beliefs—one visible, their formal beliefs, and one subterranean, their functional beliefs.

We asked students to do descriptive theological work rather than work on prescriptive theological ideas that come to them in classes and books. We asked them to take seriously their inner textbooks and to investigate them. The books we assigned and the class sessions we led certainly expressed our theological perspective, but our educational aim was to open a path for students to uncover the theology they had brought with them to seminary and into this class. Our goal was for them to connect the visible stream of what they professed to believe with the underground and hidden stream of belief that was actually shaping their lives. Our job was to create an environment, a liminal space, where they could take such a risk. These risks often led to distressing and painful emotions.

---

5. Kerr and Bowen, *Family Evaluation*.

Families: Where Theology Begins

Suffering is a theme in all the student papers I've saved from classes in three courses, including this family course. With their permission, I kept eighty-one student papers from 1984 through 1991. I drew on two of these papers in the previous chapter, and I draw on others in this one. Most papers I did not save. What caused me to choose papers with suffering as a primary thread? I saved them because they were passionately confessional. These students were unstinting in their curiosity about family relationships, which they described with intimate, detailed stories. They did not gloss over family dysfunction. They expressed painful emotion they'd kept hidden from family members and from themselves. I found in their papers troubled and contradictory accounts of their understanding of God. These students' candid accounts drew me to select their papers and not those of other students. As the writer Rita Mae Brown puts it, "Show me a writer, any writer, who hasn't suffered and I'll show you someone who writes in pastels as opposed to primary colors."[6] These papers were written in primary colors.

In our assignment for these papers, we used the terms formal theology and functional theology interchangeably with formal belief and functional belief.

SANDY'S BAGGAGE

Sandy uses the metaphor of baggage to describe her functional theology. Belonging to a family, she said, is both a blessing and a curse. After a brief reference to the blessing, she continued:

> Being part of a family means that we are cursed with a great deal of baggage for which we never asked. . . . We have no option but to shoulder the baggage of our family's past generations. The passing on of the family baggage is so subtle, and the load feels so familiar and natural, that we can be completely unaware of the heavy load we carry. . . . I am able to unload a bit of the extra weight . . . over-responsibility, misplaced guilt, etc., even though I am always finding new

---

6. Brown, *Starting from Scratch*, 31.

> bits of it here and there. Most of my baggage cannot be dumped, though. The baggage is too much a part of who I am. The spoken and unspoken messages I received from my parents, the messages they received from their parents—all these are a permanent part of my family baggage. . . . What can I do with all my stuff, then? I can evaluate and rearrange the load. . . . Somehow, it seems easier to carry a heavy package if I have some idea of what is inside. . . . This paper is somewhat of a disclosure of what I have found in my bags marked "unfinished family business."

Next she described her family over three generations and identified her role as the Golden Child:

> As the Golden Child, the Miss America, I felt it was my responsibility to save the family, even though I never thought this consciously. . . . Above all, I tried to get my parents to love one another and be kind to one another. . . . I was tireless in my zeal to save them both from each other. . . . I tried to rescue Daddy from his depression and loneliness. . . . Our entire family arranged itself around my father's depression, treating him as an emotional invalid.

Sandy's father was obsessed with the state of his relationship with God, "fearing that he was not really saved because of a sexual sin he had committed after he had been saved. Because of this he had to do right out of fear of God." About the family's theology she wrote:

> The essence of my family's functional theology could be summed up in one phrase: the importance of doing what's right. Our lives were guided by rules upon rules. . . . The message I learned about God and grace was this: God loves you and will forgive all your sins if you ask him. But, we might be mistaken about this, so we'd better try hard to be as nearly perfect (like Jesus) as possible and never do anything that might displease God, just in case we're wrong.

When Sandy was fifteen, she got into trouble because she had allowed her boyfriend to come over when no one else was at home. Her mother told her how this was not acceptable, but then she added, "Sandy, if you were ever to get pregnant (outside marriage) it would

Families: Where Theology Begins

just about kill me. But, no matter what you do, you will still be my daughter, and I will always love you." This recollection brings her to a hopeful congruence between her functional and formal theology—a gracious mother representing a gracious God. "That statement," Sandy says, "gave me great comfort and security; it still does."

Sandy was a class group facilitator, and in her group she sought to share responsibilities with other group members and keep herself from trying to do it all on her own as she'd done in her family. This wasn't easy for her. "I wanted to share in token responsibilities," she said, "but when it came to 'real' group work (whatever that is), I had to do it all." Her group challenged her for trying to control them. As she put it, they "defrocked" her, and she was angry about this coup. She said, "Talking about my anger about being defrocked . . . helped me to understand what was going on." This open expression of anger ran counter to the family's rules. "In my family negative emotions were not discussed, especially according to my mother's rules. Her ghost hovered over our group for a while. . . . I finally challenged that ghost, and then real, honest group building could begin."

The group gave Sandy a place to try out behaviors that contradicted the family's theology—behaviors such as openly expressing anger and accepting failure and imperfection. "When I came to group on April 18 without my paper," Sandy reports, "I was not tossed out as leader or rejected. I only allowed myself to do it because I felt sure of their acceptance of me. I try to believe the same is true of God, but I still carry that fear that I might be wrong."

With the help of other group members, she was able to create a safe place where she could confess her theological perplexity and doubt, disclosing another layer of her inner textbook:

> The old definitions with which I grew up no longer make sense for me, but I do not know how to replace them. What does Christ's death and resurrection mean for me? In what ways am I a "saved" person? This is an uncomfortable, frightening place for me. I feel as if I am on the edges of heresy—that I may be abandoning the faith. Yet, I must be honest with my doubts and questions when I find a safe place to do so.

TED: CONTROL AND PERFECTION

Ted led a small group in this class. Out of his inner textbook he described his family:

> In my family's quest to be ideal, we have said, "To be loved by God you must be perfect." ... What is the result of not being perfect? ... God punishes you by leaving you all alone. You must be good and to be good means always taking care of someone else's needs and denying your own needs. Evil is living selfishly. To insult someone in my family you say, "You do not care about anyone but yourself." Individuality in any form is evil in the family. Formally, we affirm God is a loving god who works in ways unknown but is always accepting us no matter what our flaws are. Functionally, we believe you must be good, take care of everyone, or the monster god will punish your lack of concern.

Ted was about eight years old when violent arguments began to break out between his parents. In these arguments, he said, "very often something would get broken."

> A countertop was hammered with a hairspray can leaving permanent rings in the wood. The stove door was slammed so hard it never remained open again by itself. A kitchen drawer was slammed so hard the front of the door cracked down the middle. A piece of the best china was broken in half... The true reason for this conflict was never expressed.

His mother developed migraine headaches during this time, and, he says, "I became triangled into my parents' relationship by my mother asking me to take care of her when she was sick."

> My mother found in me someone who would take care of her and someone she could teach not to abandon her like her father ... or [my] Dad. I became her emotional spouse in a very tightly fused relationship. Along with my role as caretaker to my mother I was also expected to be perfect. At times she forced me to be perfect in a controlling, abusive manner. I leave this statement unsupported because I am

not ready to deal with this dimension of our relationship in this paper.

In his family, Ted dealt with the challenges of being his mother's caretaker, being afraid of his parents' conflict, fearing abandonment, and the demand that he be perfect. As he considered his group facilitation task, he determined to risk more, to do so sooner than in a previous group he'd led, and "to give up some of my control and let all members share in decision-making and leadership of the group." He did well on both of these fronts, and in this group he faced the tension between his functional theology of perfection and his formal theology of grace. He said he was able to do the painful work of facing his family

> because in the group with people sharing their pain and struggles I experience Christ. A Christ that calls me and those around me to wholeness. I think about the day I presented my family and Art said, "I really feel the Lord was here today." Others in the group agreed and I replied, "I agree with Art. I felt the presence of God here as well." Our theological understanding of what this meant may have been vastly different but what we felt was the same. We had felt the Christ among us and we had been joined together in the process. I must continue with this process because this is where I find God.

JESUS AND THE CREATION OF AN ALTERNATIVE FAMILY

Both Sandy and Ted found in their small group a second family, a family different than the one in which they had grown up. They describe what ethnographers and anthropologists call a "fictive family."[7] People in fictive families are related neither by blood ties nor by marriage but rather by a spoken or unspoken covenant—a set of promises or commitments they make to each other. The small groups in my class had a written covenant, a list of promises, the

---

7. Another term for "fictive family" would be a "family of choice."

most important one being a commitment to confidentiality—not to speak to others about a member of the group unless that person gave them permission to do so. In the structure of this class, the members of Ted's group were assigned, but within that givenness group members made choices and took risks that bound them together in family-like relationships.

The group became a fictive family. Within that fictive family they dared to find ways to relate differently to one another than in their family of origin. The functional theology of Ted's family told him he must be perfect and devote his life to denying his own needs in order to serve the needs of others. He did not do that in his group. He expressed his vulnerability, imperfection, and need for care from other group members. He expressed feelings that would have been forbidden in his biological family. Although he knew there were different theological views in the group, he believed that they experienced Christ as their host and that for that time together they were Christ's family.

Sandy's and Ted's groups, and other class groups that took such risks, were playing out a narrative that relates to Jesus' subversion of the prevailing first-century cultural understanding of family relationships. He created fictive families.[8] To understand his fictive family narrative it's necessary first to grasp his attitude toward his biological family.

Mark, the earliest Gospel, begins without any reference to Jesus' family or lineage. Instead, Mark opens with, "The beginning of the good news of Jesus Christ the Son of God" (1:1). This statement is followed by the account of Jesus' baptism in which a voice from heaven says, "You are my Son, the Beloved; with you I am well pleased" (1:9–11). Mark never mentions Jesus' biological father.[9] In this Gospel, the first reference to Jesus' family is to God as his father. Jesus' other family members, according to Mark, are his mother, brothers, and sisters—no mention of a father other than God.

---

8. Poetker, "Domestic Domains," 14–23.

9. Whether or not Joseph was Jesus' father is central to the debate over Jesus' humanity. If he was fully human, did that not mean that he had a human father?

Families: Where Theology Begins

Jesus' family became alarmed when his appearances and teaching drew large crowds. What he said and did so provoked his listeners that some of them said, "He has gone out of his mind." His family set out to "take hold of him." They arrived to find him surrounded by a crowd so thick they couldn't get near him, and they sent for him. "Your mother and your brothers and sisters are outside, asking for you," he's told. His response is stunning: "'Who are my mother and my brothers?' and looking at those who sat around him he said, 'Here are my mother and my brothers! Whoever does the will of God is my brother and sister and mother.'"[10] Mark sets Jesus' biological family outside the surrounding crowd who are eager to hear Jesus' words. Excluding his biological family members, Jesus declares that those not kin to him are his family. And Mark matches this disruption of normal family relationships by reporting that Jesus called his disciples away from their homes to join his new family—a fictive kin community.

Mark does not idealize Jesus' new fictive family. These family members fail to understand Jesus' mission, are troubled by sibling rivalry, and seek privileges and power for themselves. His closest new family members renounce and betray him. Mark's account of Jesus' new family makes clear that it is flawed from the beginning. No perfection here. It is a flawed family sustained by God's ceaseless redemptive work.

Jesus subverts his disciples' expectations about traditional family relationships. He inverts the patriarchal hierarchy of the culture's family dynamics. He responds to the disciples' concern over who would have the greatest honor and power by saying, "Whoever wants to be first must be last of all and servant of all."[11] Strikingly Jesus lifts up children, who are nobodies in that culture, to represent the most fundamental quality of his new family's relationships. "He took a little child and put it among them; and taking it in his arms, he said to them, 'Whoever welcomes one such child in my name welcomes

---

10. Mark 3:20–35.
11. Mark 9:33–35.

me, and whoever welcomes me welcomes not me but the one who sent me.'"[12]

This class gave students a way to look back at themselves as children and see the vulnerability of their child selves. They brought their child selves into the fictive family groups made up of fellow students. There was no teacher in these groups, no one to whom they could relate as a parent figure. And in these fictive families they contended with the demon of perfectionism.

EVAN'S FAMILY OF PERFECTION

Although he does not use the word "fictive," Evan describes how he entered the fictive family of the groups he led in two different classes. In one group Evan was challenged by Jim "who was wanting to be the group leader.... He challenged me ... and raised my anxiety." Evan's reaction to Jim at first was defensive; however, he realized that he was reacting to Jim just the way Evan did to his father. And he made a change in his response to Jim: "I was able to experience Jim's fears of abandonment and simply to be with him as opposed to reacting to his struggle to be in control."

Evan tells a story about himself and two of his friends when he was fifteen. As they walked through parked cars on their way to a football game, one of his friends "snapped off a car radio antenna. He launched it into the air. 'Wow!' I thought, 'that looked easy.' I tentatively curved my fingers around an antenna, twisted my wrist, and it broke. Dropping it to the ground I walked on." Another student had seen his two friends committing these acts of vandalism; soon after, they were caught and arrested by a security officer.

Evan was not pursued, and he walked away hoping his friends would not tell on him. He arrived home acting as if nothing had happened. Soon the phone rang in the kitchen, and his parents were told to bring Evan to the police station. At the station, he pled his innocence but then confessed, "Well, I might have broken one off." The police officer said, "Well you just as well broke them all." When

---

12. Mark 9:36–37.

they returned home, his dad gave him a whipping, saying, "I'm going to whip you for every year you have lived."

This act of vandalism was out of character for Evan. He makes this episode central to his family story. He signals this by the way he introduces the narrative: "Visit with me an event in the life of fifteen-year-old Evan [here he uses his first, middle, and last name]." He speculates on his motive for snapping off the antenna, and then tells how he and his parents redeemed the event:

> My act of vandalism seems to have served several functions. One, it was a way of acting out Dad's "helplessness" concerning the way he had been demoted [at work]. Two, it diverted the attention from him to me. I got the attention I missed by being quiet. And, it was a way of expressing some of my anger about being emotionally abandoned by Dad. Perhaps more important than understanding all the events surrounding my act of vandalism is the fact that this event is no longer regarded as a secret. As a part of this project I asked Mom and Dad what they could remember about the event. That was the first time in seventeen years that the subject had been broached. The exciting part for me was to hear Mom's response to this event. "I always thought this was a minor event in your life," she said. I would not have heard that if the subject had not been reopened.
>
> The God worshipped by our family would not tolerate imperfection. Hence, we were constantly masking or denying mistakes and faults. The groups, however, provided an opportunity to destroy that myth.

Prompted by his work in this course, Evan went home and asked his parents about this act of vandalism—a clear case of moral failure—and his mother recast the event in one graceful sentence.

The theme of perfection is a thread that runs through all papers that I kept in this family class. Although students might confess a gracious God, their functional theology demanded perfection. The quest for perfection, driven by anxious striving, is a hallmark of the culture's conventional wisdom. In conventional cultural wisdom, everything depends on how well you perform. God is the source, enforcer, and legitimator of that quest. One student described the quest's ultimate disillusion. "My desire was to please 'God,' my family, and friends," he said. "I was well on the road to becoming 'good.'" But this path, he confessed, left him "trapped on the road to perfection."

KAY: LOVE AND PERFECTIONISM

Kay writes her paper in the form of a letter to her mother, and she connects her quest for perfection to being loved. Will her parents and God love her if she's not perfect? She writes to her mother:

> You know what bothers me about you. You are such a perfectionist. I'm a perfectionist, too; I worry if I'm not able to do everything perfectly. I tried so hard to be a good child. I guess I thought that that's why you and Daddy loved me so much. I guess somewhere deep down I wondered if you could do that if I weren't perfect. You took me to church. I learned that God loves me just because God does. Of course I say that I believe that, but it just doesn't seem quite right. How could anyone love me just because they do? How could anyone love me if they knew how imperfect I am? Trying to be perfect makes me tired.

Kay also tells how she felt isolated from her peers. She was frequently ill, saw many doctors, and was hospitalized. "Being sick at home made me even more isolated," she wrote, "but it also protected me from the risk involved in having to be a part of what was going on around me. If I risked being a part of life at school and with my friends, I might have failed. They might have found out that I wasn't perfect. I was isolated at home. I was sick, but that made me even more imperfect."

Kay related her quest for perfection to how she led her small group. "During the beginning of the semester," she wrote, "I felt a great deal of pressure to be the perfect group leader. I thought I had to have all the answers and be able to solve all the problems." As the semester unfolded, she discovered that her attempt to be a perfect leader was working against her:

I came to see that it was more valuable to the group and to me that I be myself and struggle honestly with the issues in my family. As I began to be open about where I was in the process and how I felt each day, the group was able to carry out its tasks concerning families and concerning [our group] process. . . . I think my struggle has been accepting the unconditional love and grace of God knowing that I am not perfect. I have also struggled to see God at work in my imperfect family. I have not been able to believe that my family or other people could love me unconditionally, so I have worked hard to be perfect. . . . I think through discovering unconditional love and acceptance from people around me [in my group], I will be able to accept the grace and love from God. I think that is one way that God shows us grace and love, through the people around us.

BETH: IMAGINING DISASTER

During this family class, Beth discovered that she was pregnant. Soon she learned that she might lose the baby.

"I felt that God was teasing us [her and her husband] and trying to make us pay for some unknown sin. Now that the baby seems to be okay, I still fear for his/her 'perfectness.'" She imagined that the baby will be handicapped causing her to give up her career. She imagined that then her husband will die and she will be left to support herself and the handicapped baby. "My formal theology says that God wants us to have this baby and me to have a career, but my functional theology says that God is going to take the baby, my husband, and my career away in some cruel and unjust way."

Beth makes an important shift away from this disastrous narrative about herself when she says about her family,

> Sure, things were hell a lot of the time, but there were also some good things, too. Nothing is completely all bad (or all good). For me to be honest about my family means that I must admit that there was a mix of good times and bad in the family. And just because there were some pretty rotten

> times doesn't mean that the situation isn't redeemable. . . .
> For the first time I think it's okay to admit that things were
> not okay and see something besides utter despair.

She describes how the progress she's made in understanding her family and its functional theology has enabled her to be honest with her parents "without the fear of being 'struck down.'" "They are going to love me anyway. They aren't going to fall apart if I don't continue to walk over the same egg shells of my childhood days. In fact I'm beginning to feel brave enough to stomp on those egg shells."

Despite being the leader of her small group, Beth failed to show up when it was her turn to share her family paper. Her failing to show up, she said, "was an extremely helpful time for me. It helped me evaluate my stress level and my physical condition and made me realize that I had been expecting way too much of myself." When her group didn't get angry with her for missing the group session, she was surprised. "They didn't get mad and berate me for missing the group." This event further weakened her narrative that if you aren't perfect disaster will strike.

ANITA: TAKING A RISK TO BE REAL

Anita was also on a quest for perfection. She, too, led a group in the family class. And she also had difficulty presenting her paper on her family to that group. "I felt emotionally overwhelmed by the idea of writing about my family of origin. I was beginning to feel physically ill every time I even thought about writing." It was her turn to present her paper to her group, and she hadn't written it. "I went to the group not knowing what to expect but determined to be truthful about my dilemma." She told the group about her painful resistance to writing her paper. "The day I presented my family, without my paper, was most valuable," she said, "because I experienced grace. I found that even when I had the responsibility of facilitating the group, I could honestly express my struggles and be accepted."

> My expectation was that I had to play the game exactly right
> or I would be rejected. There were rules, expectations, and

> deadlines with no room for human foibles. Yet a fear greater than facing the group kept me from writing. The fear was that if I wrote what I really felt, my life would go out of control and the unleashing of emotion would kill me. Being real was not safe in my family. On the battle line of these conflicting forces, I experienced grace in my group. When I was most confused and least expected it, I was given a safe place—permission to be real.

She learned, as other group leaders did, that confessing her failure to do the assignment perfectly as prescribed actually helped the group move to a deeper level of sharing and risk taking. She said, "It was as if the others only needed an indication that such sharing was appropriate."

She described the power of the family's theology of perfection and how, although her group helped her find a graceful alternative to it, she nonetheless continued to be haunted by it. In her family, she said,

> we had to pretend; we could not be real. I worked so hard to be in control at all times that I did not have a reality other than that focused on stabilizing the family image.... One critical rule was that no one should talk about what was really happening.... My family focused on Daddy's alcoholism as a reason for ignoring the rest of the family pain. Another rule was that everything was somebody's fault. I assumed that many things were my fault. I was taught to believe in this all-powerful, all-loving god who was going to be there for me; however, I really believed that I couldn't count on anyone else, and if things were going to get done, I would have to do them myself. Even now, god does not feel real to me. For now, I am trying to accept that I am in a place of not believing and yet not knowing. I am aware that I am on a journey. I am beginning to understand that normal is not knowing. How could I know? I do not easily face my finitude.... The struggle continues between the real me and the fabricated, masked performer who avoids the fear and pain and limitations at all costs.

LOSING THE PATINA OF PERFECTION

Margaret, who also led one of the groups, wrote,

> In our small groups, everybody wanted to be successful. All of us started out with this patina[13] in place: "I'm going to be sensitive. I'm going to be forthcoming but not too forthcoming. We're going to be intimate, but it's not going to get messy. I'm going to be sort of pristine in the way that I handle this." I knew how I wanted to be perceived, and other people in the group wanted the same thing. And all of us were posturing. But you really can't do that if you tell your story. The papers we wrote got underneath our presenting patina. Then in the group we had to talk about our paper and tell more of the story. And there's something so potent and subversive about telling our story and listening to others tell their stories. I think it was a two-pronged thing. If you're telling the truth about your own life, the patina comes off. And if you have a safe small group listening to you, or a safe person, everybody's changed. You simply couldn't walk out of one of those meetings, if people were telling the truth, and not be changed. I really believe that.
>
> Then we would come into the leadership group, and we would tell the truth about things that were going on in our groups. Sometimes we were hitting home runs. Sometimes we were failing. Sometimes really scary things happened in the groups, and that seemed to me to make the group experience more real. I don't know that anybody was able to get through a whole semester in the leaders' group with this patina on. If they did, they were failing. I gained a sense that success was being able to take that patina off and tell the truth and be able to fail.

Students whose stories I report in this book discovered events from their past that had lain undisturbed in their inner textbooks until they were called forth by assignments in my classes. What they found in their stories, and in mine, was the raw material of our functional theology.

---

13. Patina is a film on metal or wood that develops over time.

Families: Where Theology Begins

FAMILIES, BIOLOGICAL AND FICTIVE

Families write the first draft of the inner textbooks we carry with us the rest of our lives. These inner texts contain both our formal beliefs—what we consciously believe—and our functional beliefs—those hidden convictions that frequently override what we consciously profess. In this chapter we have heard from students who had the courage to explore these contending theological forces.

The peer-led groups in these classes became fictive families that often transcended the power of students' biological families and made possible a revealing examination of the conflict between their formal and functional beliefs. These fictive family groups have some kinship with the groups of people Jesus called his family—people he gathered, often around meals, for intimate conversation—fictive families that transcended the hierarchical, patriarchal family structure of first-century Roman and Jewish biological families.

THE KEYS

Narratives that students tell about themselves in this chapter report the hard work they are doing to understand the formal and functional beliefs of the families in which they grew up. In the small groups of the class, they have a place to tell the stories, *the narratives*, that have come out of this hard work.

Belonging takes place naturally as these students share their stories. The vulnerability of these stories creates bonds of care and support between the members of the group. Personal narratives connect these group members to each other.

Diversity and Whiteness do not appear in the stories in this chapter. They are notable by their absence. These students and their teachers were all White. And it's probably the case that none of us were aware of our Whiteness or that it was an issue for us.

As these students worked to understand the functional theology in their families of origin, and as they told their story of this work in their group, they could go only so far in reporting their discoveries.

They were on the edge of what they could take in and tell about. Anita described the experience as a fear that if she wrote what she really felt "the unleashing of emotion would kill me." She was at the brink of the ineffable. Once she faced this terror, she was able, she said, to be real in her group.

QUESTIONS

1. Do you think that the personal vulnerability and self-discovery described in this chapter have a legitimate place in theological education? If so, why? If not, why not?
2. If Black/White diversity wasn't part of this class, what other diversity do you see in it?
3. In what ways has the quest for perfection interfered with your learning or your teaching?
4. What story do you have that reveals the tension between your formal beliefs and your functional beliefs?
5. Do you have any family stories of sundown towns?

6

The Power of Belonging
Education with Peer-Led Student Groups

> Theological education must capture its central work—to form us in the
> art of cultivating belonging.
>
> —WILLIE JAMES JENNINGS[1]

THIS STATEMENT BY WILLIE James Jennings challenges the banking hermeneutic of Western education which, in its concern for content, gives little attention to belonging. I have, in my life as an educator, pursued a hermeneutic of belonging. The emotional, intellectual, spiritual, and relational power in the student-led groups I have described in chapters 3 and 5 and will tell about in this chapter grows out of their intense experiences of belonging. One test of the enduring value of belonging as the central work of theological education (although the test isn't a systematic one) is asking students some thirty years later what they recall about the courses and their participation in these groups. You have heard from some of these students, now middle-aged adults. Their experience in these courses, in these groups, has influenced their lives well into middle adulthood.

---

1. Jennings, *After Whiteness*, 10.

A HERMENEUTIC OF BELONGING AS MANIFEST IN STUDENT-LED PEER GROUPS

A hermeneutic of belonging begins with the person of the teacher and calls for teachers to make their own self understanding an integral part of their teaching. If I am teaching a course on family process, for example, then I need in one way or another to tell students the story of my experience in the family in which I grew up. Teachers, whether they know it or not, bring their own story into their teaching, and students deserve to know something about it.

This hermeneutic of belonging also requires that teachers cultivate *an empathic curiosity*. I enter a classroom of thirty students the first day of the semester, and as I survey this group I am concerned to know their stories—who are they and what brought them to this school and then to this class? What formative experiences have prepared them for this educational venture? What do they already know about the subject matter of the course?

A third dimension of this hermeneutic of belonging is how to make it possible for these students to connect their story with the subject matter of this course. If I am teaching about Jesus' parables, for example, what problem can I pose for students that will open a way for them to relate their story to a parable of Jesus? In chapter 3 you've read accounts of students who did that—relating three early childhood memories to a parable of Jesus.

What follows is an expanded version of my hermeneutic of belonging. It addresses these questions: What is my own story of belonging to groups? How do you create a climate of trust in which students feel safe to tell their stories? How does the metaphor of pilgrimage describe the emotional, spiritual, and intellectual journey that can occur in these groups? How can a teaching team create a belonging environment? And how would these groups have been different if they had been racially diverse?

The Power of Belonging

MY STORY OF FORMING AND BELONGING TO GROUPS

I have been a member of a men's group that has lasted almost fifty years. The usual membership has been seven. During the life of the group, three of us moved away and two members died. Twice the group added two new members to fill vacancies. At the beginning we were a group of pastoral counselors. We organized as a case conference where we would take turns presenting our work with clients. Before long we realized that *we were our cases* and that *we* needed therapy about as much as our clients did. For the most part we set aside client cases and focused on our own stories. We met twice a month for two hours. I moved away and was absent from the group for a period of five years while I lived in Atlanta and then for ten years following my retirement move to Matthews, North Carolina. I have now rejoined the group by way of Zoom where six of us sign in from three different cities.

What was so valuable about the group that it lasted almost five decades? It was a place for us to talk about our lives in a way we could not talk about them anywhere else. We supported each other through marital problems, divorces, remarriages, illnesses, deaths of parents and siblings, crises where we worked, and misadventures of our children. We told stories about our successes and our failures, our depression and our anxiety, our hopes and our fears.

Conflicts occurred within the group, but they never fractured it. Even after they were resolved, however, some conflicts hung around the edges of the group and intruded from time to time.

As trust developed in the group (and this took time), I was more and more able to tell my companions about my inner life—my hopes, my successes and failures, my worries, my fears, and my troubled relationships. I remember talking about my relationship with my mother, who suffered from dementia and for whom I had arranged a place in a nursing home. I talked about how difficult it was to visit her because we were so emotionally tied together—me, her only child—and how distressing it was to see her in her demented condition. As I talked about this in our group one day, Charles looked over at me and said, "I would be glad to visit your mother." Hearing this unexpected, out-of-the-blue response, I broke down and cried. I almost never cry, but I did here. And in this flow of tears I felt an immense relief. As it turned out, I didn't really expect him to visit her. And he never did. But that wasn't what mattered. What did matter was his empathy and his ability in that moment to understand and touch my painful feelings. A year or so later, he was visiting his own mother who was near death, and I was supporting him as he told about his visits to be with her.

My investment in groups began in my seminary classes at The Southern Baptist Theological Seminary in pastoral care and in clinical pastoral education in hospital settings. It continued during my graduate work where each semester I served as a group facilitator for students in the basic course in pastoral care. I experienced the power of these groups for self-discovery and change. As I facilitated these groups I had feelings of self-fulfillment I had not known before. These group experiences gave me a life-long investment in facilitating small groups and belonging to a peer group. I formed or participated in a regular support group wherever we lived.

When I was a pastor in Gainesville, Florida, from 1967 to 1970, I pulled together a group of clergy, and we met weekly. I belonged to the group of pastoral counselors I described above when I lived near Raleigh in Wake Forest, from 1977 to 1991. When I moved to Atlanta in 1991, I formed a support group there. When I returned to Raleigh in 1996, I rejoined the Raleigh group. And when I moved to Matthews, near Charlotte, in 2012, I formed a support group of clergy there which, at the time this book is published, is still meeting.

I wanted and needed a group, a fictive family, wherever I lived. In addition to these groups, I established the narrative therapy seminar at Triangle Pastoral Counseling and participated in it from 1997 to 2012. In this seminar I developed what was for me my most satisfying group structure. I describe that in the next chapter.

The Power of Belonging

PARKER PALMER'S CIRCLES OF TRUST

In 2002 I was co-director of a Sustaining Pastoral Excellence project, and found that Parker Palmer gave us valuable guidance about how to lead the groups of clergy in our project. His understanding of group process reinforced the attributes of groups that I sought to develop in my classes and in the groups I have led or to which I have belonged after ending my teaching career.[2]

In circles of trust, the main work is to release the power of each member's *inner teacher*—that reservoir of wisdom within persons that can guide them in solving their problems and fulfilling their aspirations. Parker Palmer's *inner teacher* is very close to what I call one's *inner textbook*.

For Palmer, groups that draw out one's inner teacher (or inner textbook) follow a basic rule of "No fixing, no saving, no advising, no setting each other straight."[3] When members follow this rule and refrain from trying to fix each other, they make room for the inner teacher to appear. The task of the group is to "hold each other in a space where the soul feels safe enough to speak its truth—and we feel safe enough to become more receptive to the implications of that truth for our lives."[4] Palmer uses the term "soul" almost interchangeably with "inner teacher." The soul, he says, is like a wild animal:

> Like a wild animal, the soul is tough, resilient, resourceful, savvy, and self-sufficient: it knows how to survive in hard places. I learned about these qualities during my bouts with depression. In that deadly darkness, the faculties I had always depended on collapsed. My intellect was useless; my emotions were dead; my will was impotent; my ego was shattered. But from time to time, deep in the thickets of my inner wilderness, I could sense the presence of something

---

2. Palmer, *Hidden Wholeness*.
3. Palmer, *Hidden Wholeness*, 114.
4. Palmer, *Hidden Wholeness*, 122.

that knew how to stay alive even when the rest of me wanted to die. That something was my tough and tenacious soul.[5]

Palmer goes on to say that despite being so tough, the soul is also shy. It is just like a wild animal that seeks safety in the underbrush in the presence of other people. If people go crashing through the forest looking for it, then it hides. Then he describes what a support group should not do, and that is to be helpful. Being helpful too often comes in the form of teaching, advising, cajoling, persuading, or otherwise trying to solve somebody else's problem. So long as that is happening, the soul stays hidden; and the wisdom, care, and direction the soul can offer the person remains untapped.

Palmer says it's important to observe the difference between *instrumental* and *expressive* speech. Everyday speech is instrumental. It seeks to achieve a goal, to fix things or get things the way we want, rather than to express one's truth. When we speak expressively, however, we're not trying to teach or fix but to give the inner teacher an opportunity to teach us. We are speaking from our inward center and listening to others who do the same. It is not easy to speak expressively without sliding over into speaking instrumentally.

> The signs that we are speaking *from* that inward center are subtle, as subtle as the stillness of a pond; the capacity to recognize them grows slowly as we speak in a space where no one is making ripples. . . . When we speak directly to others in order to achieve a goal, we feel the anxiety that comes from trying to exercise influence. But when we speak . . . free of the need to achieve a result—we feel energized and at peace. Now we speak with no other motive than to tell the truth.[6]

GROUPS CREATING LIMINAL SPACE

I believe that peer-led groups are a valuable key to successful teaching and learning because they facilitate belonging. In these groups

5. Palmer, *Hidden Wholeness*, 58.
6. Palmer, *Hidden Wholeness*, 119.

students risk opening their inner textbooks and relate what they find there to the content of the course. The groups that succeeded in this endeavor did so because they were able to create a liminal space together.

What is a liminal space? For anthropologist Victor Turner, liminality or liminal space is a dimension of ritual. Ritual, he says, is a recurring human activity that meets the perennial need of human society to transcend the limitations of social structure.[7] He defines ritual as "planned or improvised performance that effects a transition from everyday life to an alternative framework within which the everyday is transformed."[8] In ritual activity, persons cross a threshold—a *limen*—and enter liminal space and time in which the usual structures of life are suspended.

Ritual process, Turner says, leads to social change. It has the power to suspend social norms, to criticize social structures, to present alternatives, and to transform existing social structures. Ritual has a subversive potential over against established practices.[9]

The liminal phase of ritual, according to Turner, can generate great power and creative energy. He speaks of "the attributes of liminal people" that include their being betwixt and between laws, customs, conventions, and status distinctions. They have crossed a threshold out of structured, differentiated, hierarchical systems into an unstructured, undifferentiated communion of equal individuals—a state of what he calls *communitas*.

PILGRIMAGE AS A METAPHOR FOR GROUP EXPERIENCE

Turner viewed pilgrimages as rich experiences of liminality and communitas. He quotes Malcolm X's description of his pilgrimage to Mecca as an example of the power a pilgrimage can engender:

---

7. Alexander, *Victor Turner Revisited*, 27–28.
8. Alexander, "Pentecostal Possession," 21.
9. Alexander, *Victor Turner Revisited*, 29–33.

> On this pilgrimage, what I have seen and experienced has forced me to *rearrange* much of my thought-patterns previously held. . . . During the past eleven days here in the Muslim world, I have eaten from the same plate, drunk from the same glass, and slept in the same bed (or on the same rug)—while praying *to the same God* . . . with fellow Muslims, whose eyes were the bluest of blue, whose hair was the blondest of blond, and whose skin was the whitest of white. And in the *words* and in the *actions* and in the *deeds* of the "white" Muslims, I felt the same sincerity that I had felt among the black African Muslims of Nigeria, Sudan, and Ghana. We were *truly* . . . all the same (brothers)—because their belief in one God had removed the "white" from their *minds*, the "white" from their *behavior*, and the "white" from their *attitude*.[10]

With Malcolm X's striking description of his pilgrimage to Mecca, I venture this hypothesis: that Victor Turner's understanding of liminality, communitas, and pilgrimage offers a perspective for interpreting the experiences of students in the small groups in my classes. Turner's view certainly would not characterize every one of these groups. But it would, I believe, characterize the groups of those students whose papers I have drawn upon for this book.

Features of Turner's understanding of pilgrimage as it applies to peer-led groups in my courses would include the following:[11]

- *Pilgrims go on a journey outside the usual structures of everyday life to find out who they really are.* Many of the students in peer-led groups, as they explore their early childhood memories or the theology of their family of origin, take an emotional and cognitive journey different from what usually occurs in their academic experience. This journey takes them out of the familiar structure and practices of formal education and into unexplored personal territory where they find things that may trouble them

---

10. Turner, *Dramas, Fields, and Metaphors*, 168–69, quoting X, *Autobiography of Malcolm X*, 340–41. (All of the italicized emphases are by Malcolm X.)

11. Turner, *Dramas, Fields, and Metaphors*, 182–212.

and things that may inspire them—but almost always discover things they didn't know they had within their inner textbooks.

- *This journey takes them into unexpected experiences where they are supported by communitas and comradeship.* It is difficult to overestimate the value and power of well-run student peer groups. Such groups move students away from banking education where the main experience is receiving information. These peer groups offer an intimacy and personal engagement that cannot happen in classes that have no small group component.

- *Those journeying on the pilgrimage enter into a liminal experience that is "in and out of time" with the possibility of inward transformation of spirit or personality.* One of the student group facilitators recalls an encounter with me that she says has had a lasting effect. This occurred during the time that I was the president of the Southeastern Seminary chapter of the American Association of University Professors and had been hard at work leading the faculty to challenge the takeover of the seminary by fundamentalist trustees. The encounter took place in the seminar for group facilitators. In an interview some thirty years later, this is what she recalls:

> I remember your saying something in a kind of beleaguered way about "I can't do everything." And I said, "Well, nobody asked you to." And, you know, one of those fortunate things that flies out of your mouth before you have a chance to stop yourself. And then I had to hold on to myself. And you were really angry. And it really was a learning that shaped the rest of my life because I didn't die, and I didn't lose favor with you. It felt like walking on a razor's edge. Was I right? was I wrong? I didn't know. But the fact that you reacted the way that you did and that the tension mushroomed so fast in the room told me that I might have been right. I was impertinent and knew I had hit a nerve. So now I'm so grateful that it happened because I didn't die.

She went on to enter a career as a therapist, becoming a leader in a therapy practice. And in this practice she earned a reputation for telling the unvarnished truth when it was needed—just as she had done with me in that seminar years earlier.

- *The journey may involve the "negation of many features of preliminal social structure and affirmation of another order of things and relations."*[12] Recall from chapter 3 Jeff's response to me thirty years after that class, "I would say the class altered my view of God. In fact, it altered my world view. At that point God and I parted ways. Yet, I continue to feel some connection to what I would call the ineffable."

  In such a group, on such a pilgrimage, participants could discover how to transcend the confining boundaries of caste and learn how to form intimate relationships with members of another caste/race. What we read above from Malcolm X about his pilgrimage to Mecca is convincing testimony to this possibility—one more reason to ensure that these groups are interracial. The groups in my classes were not interracial, and this was a regrettable deficiency.

- *A pilgrimage into the unknown arouses anxiety which is contained and managed by the support and understanding of fellow pilgrims.* The work on these assignments produces anxiety for which the student needed the comradeship, the communitas, of fellow travelers. In chapter 5 we heard Sandy confess,

  > The old definitions with which I grew up no longer make sense for me, but I do not know how to replace them. What *does* Christ's death and resurrection mean for me? In what ways am I a "saved" person? This is an uncomfortable, frightening place for me. I feel as if I am on the edges of heresy—that I may be abandoning the faith. Yet, I must be honest with my doubts and questions when I find a safe place to do so.

  That safe place was her peer group.

---

12. Turner, *Dramas, Fields, and Metaphors*, 196.

- *Differences of belief and views among the pilgrims are not eliminated, "but the sting of divisiveness is removed" and "differences are accepted or tolerated rather than aggravated into grounds of aggressive opposition."*[13] In chapter 5, we read about Evan, as a group leader, being challenged by a member who competed with him to be the group leader. At first Evan was defensive, but then he realized that he was reacting to Jim just the way he did to his father, and changed course. "I was able to experience Jim's fears of abandonment," he said, "and simply to be with him as opposed to reacting to his struggle to be in control."

- *On the journey most pilgrims experience healing.* Some students reported healing between themselves and their parents when they went home and ventured to relate to their parents differently than in the past or told their parents what they discovered about the meaning and significance of early family experiences. Angela worked hard on her relationship with her mother in her paper and in her peer group, as she told in chapter 5. It was a difficult and painful venture. At the end of her semester paper, she told of going home for the weekend and was able to look more honestly at her mother. This meant that she had been able to let go of relating to her mother as a deity for whom she had to sacrifice everything. She said, "I went away feeling more secure and more loved than I ever had before, when I was trying to live up to some kind of standard. I love my mama and I am glad that now I can see her as a human, a fellow struggler rather than a god."

Victor Turner's description of pilgrimage provides a perspective for understanding the experience of the students as pilgrims on a journey. What follows is a view of this process from the perspective of the course structure and the teaching team that I developed.

---

13. Turner, *Dramas, Fields, and Metaphors*, 208.

A TEACHING TEAM THAT MADE PILGRIMAGE EXPERIENCES WORK

By the late 1980s I used small groups as part of virtually all my classes. That meant that the classes were taught and groups were overseen by a teaching team. Teaching with a team in this way is contrary to traditional banking education. These are some of the differences:

- *The professor and group leaders create a learning network that replaces the usual teacher-student dyad.* The core of this network was the group process seminar where I and peer group leaders formed our own learning community. At every seminar session group leaders brought in their leadership experiences, and the teacher's job was to facilitate their connecting these experiences with knowledge about group process. The seminar gave me a weekly reading on the wellbeing of the groups and showed me where my attention was needed. However, these student group leaders did such a good job of group facilitation that when a crisis arose in someone's group all I had to do was invite the seminar members to ask useful questions. That usually led to some resolution of the problem.

- *The basic learning strategy of these courses was to help students investigate their inner textbooks and to relate what they found there to the subject matter of the class.* In the peer groups they had a place to open their inner textbooks to tell the stories of what they discovered. In banking education, students do not open their inner textbooks because the teacher views the educational task to be making deposits of information in the student's mind. It's basically a one-way transmission process.

- *In these groups, learning occurred at many levels, and much of it took place between peers as they shared their work on the assignment of the semester paper.* By contrast, banking education operates on one level of learning—teachers providing information to mostly passive students. Even when the teacher invites class discussion, the teacher generally has the final word.

- *Students were given a problem to solve as their basic learning experience*—for example: "Establish a relationship between your three earliest childhood memories and a parable of Jesus," or "Explore the formal and functional beliefs in your family of origin." This was unlike banking education in which students receive information filtered and organized by the teacher. As they worked on their own problem, they also helped others in their group explore their problem.

- *Peer group leaders created a holding environment that provided safety for the pilgrimage.* It included (1) setting clear boundaries of beginning and ending on time and the expectation that members who had to be absent would communicate this prior to the group meeting; (2) following ground rules that protected members from being judged, admonished, or advised; that kept them from interrupting each other; and that assured that members got their fair share of air time; (3) protecting the privacy of each member with an agreement of confidentiality. Banking education seldom gives attention to the social interaction among the students in the class, not to mention ground rules for class member interaction.

THE UNTAPPED POWER OF RACIALLY DIVERSE GROUPS

The women and men in the groups I have described in this chapter were all White. What difference does that make in what I have written? A year ago I would not even have asked that question. Now I must ask, "What if every group had included both Black and White students to explore their earliest memories or to inquire into the theology of the family in which they grew up?"

On March 5, 2021, Amanda Gorman, the poet who read her poem at the inauguration of President Joe Biden, sent out this tweet. "A security guard tailed me on my walk home tonight. He demanded if I lived there because 'you look suspicious.' I showed him my keys

& buzzed myself into my building. He left, no apology. This is the reality of black girls: One day you're called an icon, the next day, a threat."[14]

In an interview with the *Washington Post* the day of the inauguration, the interviewer asked Gorman: "I know that many of your poems have strong political content. What's your first political memory?" Gorman replied,

> No one's ever asked me that before! My first political memory? I would say it wouldn't be anything like being at a protest or anything like that. It would be: When I was really young my mother would read me my Miranda Rights and made sure I knew them. My mom was not playing around. When you are a Black child growing up in America, our parents have to have what's called "the talk" with us. Except it's not about the birds and the bees and our changing bodies, it's about the potential destruction of our bodies. My mom wanted to make sure I was prepared to grow up with Black skin in America, and that was my first awakening to the political climate I was stepping into.[15]

Amanda Gorman's experience with the security guard is an all too familiar event for African Americans. If this could happen to the African American woman who recited her poem at a presidential inauguration, and if African Americans were part of the groups in these classes, their stories of being viewed as criminal suspects without cause would surely come up. And stories of racial oppression would be woven into group members' inquiry into early childhood memories and the family's beliefs. It is unlikely that any White students would be reporting early memories of their parents teaching them their Miranda Rights; however, they *would* hear it from their Black companions.

Greg Lee is a United Methodist Minister, a friend of mine, and African American. I asked Greg what he thought about my statements on race at the conclusion of this chapter. He said,

---

14. Iati, "Inaugural Poet Amanda Gorman."
15. Knox, "Amanda Gorman's First Political Memory."

The lens through which we look at things influences our perspective, and the lens in these all-White groups is less than optimal because it lacks diversity. To have Black members in these groups would open up the lens. The purpose of the class assignments is for students to search themselves. Without the Black voices, part of themselves goes unexplored. Moreover, the work in these groups calls for students to stand in each others shoes. White students standing in the shoes of Black students would open up a view of the world—and of themselves—they would never see otherwise.

THE KEYS

This chapter attempts to show how *belonging* is the key to moving education away from banking information in lecture settings to belonging in peer-led groups. I have drawn on the teacher Parker Palmer and the anthropologist Victor Turner for understanding the dynamics of these peer-led groups. In these groups students learn primarily through *narrative* as they relate to each other as they explore the subject matter of the course.

Amanda Gorman's account of being taught her Miranda Rights by her mother and of being stopped by a security guard who was suspicious of her raises a flag about *the lack of diversity* in the small groups in my classes. As a Black person, she experienced discrimination, suspicion, and threat. Without persons of color in these groups these kinds of encounters and the fear of such encounters would seldom be reported. Group members in my classes were therefore deprived of such testimony and the enlightenment it would bring.

Finally, what in these groups touched on *the ineffable*? As they lay aside the usual, familiar experiences that structure their lives, participants became open to inarticulate ways of being and of relating to other group members.

Recall the woman who, in a supervisory seminar for group leaders, said to me, "Well, nobody is asking you to," in response to my beleaguered complaint, "I can't do everything." She reports, "And then I had to hold on to myself. And it really was a learning that shaped the rest of my life because I didn't die, and I didn't lose favor with you. . . . So now I'm so grateful that it happened because I didn't die." These words point to the ineffable—that which is beyond words—what happens when you expect to die but don't?

In Malcolm X's description of his pilgrimage to Mecca and his encounter with White people who have religious experiences very much like his own, his words can carry him only so far. Beyond his words is experience that is inexpressible, ineffable. That's what can happen in liminal space.

QUESTIONS

1. To what interracial groups have you belonged? How have they been different from groups to which you belonged that were made up of only your race or ethnic group?
2. Could Victor Turner's understanding of ritual—his concepts of *liminality* and *communitas*—describe any of your teaching or learning experiences?
3. Have you ever been on a pilgrimage? If so, which of the qualities I've described in this chapter did it have?
4. What's been your experience in peer-led groups? What made a group go well? What made a group go badly?
5. Do you find the metaphors of *inner textbook* and *inner teacher* useful? Do they describe any of your experiences?

7

Narrative Means to Educational Ends

No wonder I was attracted to narrative therapy. I had been doing narrative work in the seminary classes in which I asked students to relate their earliest childhood memories to a parable of Jesus. And I had done narrative work in classes where I'd engaged students to distinguish between the formal and functional theology in their families of origin. Narrative therapy showed me that I was pursuing a narrative form of education, and it gave me a theory that brought several strands of my teaching strategy together.

At the same time, narrative therapy led me to take a much more collaborative role in the educational process. The familiar teaching role that I had enjoyed for twenty-one years ended when I left Southeastern Seminary.[1] Teaching was my passion and a large part of my identity. How would I teach now? I found my way into teaching outside academia. In this process, I gradually moved from seeing myself as a professor to seeing myself as a collaborative learner.

---

1. Southeastern Baptist Theological Seminary is one of six seminaries supported and controlled by the Southern Baptist Convention (SBC). In 1987 the SBC succeeded in placing a majority of biblical inerrantists in control of the school's board of trustees. I, along with most of the faculty, departed from the school after several years of open opposition. That, however, is another story.

WHAT IS NARRATIVE THERAPY?

Narrative therapy gives attention to the little narratives of the everyday life of clients. It begins with this knowledge, works within it, and asks questions to enlarge it. It trusts that persons seeking help have the necessary knowledge and wisdom to find their way out of their problem—*their problem-saturated story*. The work of the therapist, therefore, is to create an environment for that knowledge and wisdom to come forth. Therapists do this by taking a not-knowing position with clients and holding their own knowledge in check. The not-knowing position puts the therapist in a position of curiosity. Rather than imparting ideas or guiding clients to investigate the causes of their problems, the therapy moves forward with the therapist's curious questions. The questions invite clients to find alternative narratives in their experience that challenge the problem story they have brought into therapy. As the more desired alternative stories are brought to light, these narratives weaken the power of the problem story.

    A narrative therapy perspective in teaching leads an educator like myself to create a learning climate in which students can access their own wisdom—their own inner textbooks—to examine how the knowledge and understanding they bring with them to class can relate to the subject matter of the course. The student narratives in the previous chapters reveal that this opening of the inner textbooks leads students to find neglected but preferred parts of their story that have been hidden from their view.

MICHAEL WHITE AND DAVID EPSTON, THE FIRST NARRATIVE THERAPISTS: TAPPING THE RESOURCE OF UNSTORIED EXPERIENCES

Michael White, an Australian family therapist, led the early development of narrative therapy in the 1980s. He and his colleague from New Zealand, David Epston, co-authored *Narrative Means to*

Therapeutic Ends in 1990, the first text on narrative therapy.[2] White and Epston each worked with aboriginal peoples in Australia and New Zealand, and this influenced their appreciation for the social, cultural, and political issues that affect marginalized individuals and groups. White began his therapy work as a psychiatric social worker at Adelaide Children's Hospital. From there he established the Dulwich Centre. David Epston estimates that the books White has authored or co-authored have sold well over one hundred thousand copies in eleven languages as narrative therapy attracted a following of therapists like me.

PROBLEM-SATURATED STORIES

White and Epston speak of *problem-saturated stories* to describe how a person or a family gets locked into a difficulty, and all they can see is the problem. Narrative therapists invite clients to consider that their problem-saturated story is never the whole story.[3] Alternative narratives always exist—although they may be hidden from view. The problem-saturated story lives in a broad landscape of unstoried experiences. The narrative therapist—leading with curious questions—invites clients to draw from those unstoried experiences accounts that are exceptions to the problem story.

The unstoried experiences with which clients can counter their problem-saturated stories, however, have often been hidden from view by cultural and political narratives that want these alternative narratives to remain hidden. What are these cultural and political narratives and how do they work?

THE SOCIAL AND POLITICAL PERSPECTIVE OF NARRATIVE THERAPY

Michael White drew many of his central ideas from the French philosopher Michel Foucault and Foucault's understanding of the

---

2. White and Epston, *Narrative Means*.
3. White and Epston, *Narrative Means.*, 55–63.

relationship between power and knowledge, and how power and knowledge are used as a form of social control.[4]

Michael White wrote the first chapter of his and Epston's text, and, with the help of Michel Foucault, he describes the social, cultural, and political conditions that contribute to the problem-saturated narratives that clients bring into therapy. In this chapter, White's ideas are woven tightly together with those of Foucault. The following ideas arise from this partnership.

- We are subject to the power of "normalizing truths" that shape our lives and our relationships. These normalizing truths, propagated by those holding political power, subjugate us into conformity to their global truth claims.

- A cluster of subjugating, normalizing truths constitute a *discourse*. A discourse is a way of thinking, speaking, and acting that tells us what is "normal," what is "expected," what is "permitted." However, a discourse operates at such a fundamental level that it is not easy to detect.

- This subjugation by normalizing truths is the product of knowledge and power. Foucault views them as inseparable, often referring to them together as power/knowledge. We are all caught up in this web of power/knowledge, and it is impossible to act apart from it. We simultaneously are influenced by this power/knowledge and influence others with it.

- We cannot escape from the subjugating forces of knowledge and power. Therefore, we need to create conditions in which we can critique our own practices that are produced by this power/knowledge. Narrative therapists join their clients in the effort to challenge these subjugating powers. Such challenges are invariably political in nature.

- The techniques of power/knowledge that seek to subjugate persons to global claims of "truth" include such strategies as

---

4. Foucault, *Power/Knowledge*. This is only one source among the eight texts from which Michael White drew Foucault's ideas for chapter 1 of *Narrative Means to Therapeutic Ends*.

requiring certain people to be organized in prescribed spaces, requirements for registration and classification, requirements that exclude groups of persons, techniques for ascribing negative or restrictive identity to groups, isolating groups, and employing methods of surveillance to maintain control.

- In order to subvert these subjugating practices, narrative therapy seeks to externalize the problem—separating the problem from the person. The problem then can be viewed as an entity to be investigated with such questions as:

"What does the problem require for its survival?"

"How does the problem operate to insure a person's subjugation to it?"

"What claims does the problem make on the person, and how legitimate are those claims?"

- Once such questions can be answered, then the client and therapist can look for those instances when a person could have been subjugated to the power/knowledge of the dominant discourse but did not capitulate to it. This is the search for exceptions to what may first appear to be the absolute control of the discourse. With questions from the narrative therapist the client can begin to assemble a cluster of stories that are exceptions to the dominant discourse—weaving them into an alternative narrative to the problem-saturated one.

THE DISCOURSE OF WHITENESS: THE DEMAND FOR ITS PRESERVATION AT ALL COST

When I wrote the first version of this book, I was under the spell of *the discourse of Whiteness*. That discourse kept me from seeing that although I talked about conventional wisdom as a problem from which I sought to free myself and my students, I could not see that my Whiteness was a part of my discourse, my conventional wisdom, my way of seeing the world, and that this Whiteness discourse offered me remarkable privileges that Black people and other people of color don't have.

The cataclysmic events in the spring of 2020—the stark, vivid video recording of the death of George Floyd with the knee of police officer Derek Chauvin on his neck, the reigniting of the Black Lives Matter movement, Benjamin Boswell's project on Whiteness, the storming of the nation's Capitol propelled by a president determined to protect and preserve Whiteness at any cost, and a Supreme Court decision overturning Roe v. Wade, the most harmful effect of which fell on Black women—*these events externalized my book manuscript so that I was able to see its absolute Whiteness.* It became a problem separate from me. I then was able to see that I had to rewrite it.

Studies of race in America have located the issue of race in the social, cultural, and political disadvantage of Black persons, the question being, "What can we White people do to improve the situation of Black people?" Whiteness studies have begun to shift the focus so the question becomes, "What can we White people do to understand our Whiteness and change ourselves so that we no longer oppress Black people?"

In a three-stage process, the acquisition of Whiteness superiority begins with *signification*—the treatment of dark skinned people as inferior by the way language and custom are used. The next step in the development of Whiteness superiority is *domination*—the control of resources so that Whites are given advantages and Black people are deprived of resources. The final social step in the acquisition of Whiteness superiority is *legitimation*—the development of laws, rules, and regulations that institutionalize racism. It follows that if White identity, Whiteness, defines itself in opposition to "inferior" others, then racism is necessary to maintain White identity. In this process race in America has become a way of understanding reality.[5]

---

5. Guess, "Social Construction of Whiteness," 663–65. Guess is drawing on the work of Giddens, *Constitution of Society*.

If we come to understand the discourse of Whiteness superiority, then we are able to see that the race problem is located within us White people and not within Black persons. And if we are to deal with it, we must externalize this Whiteness to see it for what it is.

THE PRACTICE OF NOT KNOWING

I turn now from these social and political aspects of narrative therapy and their implications for understanding race and caste to give attention to other dimensions of narrative therapy and narrative education. In narrative therapy and in teaching, I had to learn how to take a not-knowing position with clients and with students. My knowing needed to be suspended in order for clients and students to have space to search their own knowledge. Narrative therapist Harlene Anderson writes *that from a not-knowing position a therapist is driven not so much by a search for the truth as by a desire to understand.*[6] We don't abandon what we know, but we suspend it in order to understand and respect the world of a client. We do not rush the process of understanding the other person. We take time to be curious. Not-knowing puts us in a place to learn what we do not know. And as we expose ourselves to what we really don't know, we open ourselves to revising what we think we know.[7] Anderson observes that

> a turn to not-knowing makes therapy, and the questions in therapy, different from traditional diagnostic exploration. If we truly do not know, then we must learn. If we attempt to learn, then we attempt to understand what the client is telling us. Knowing and understanding in this mode are *always on the way*. A therapist must risk being a learner again with each client—a very humbling and freeing experience.[8]

---

6. Anderson, *Conversation, Language, and Possibilities*, 141.
7. Anderson, *Conversation, Language, and Possibilities*, 134–40.
8. Anderson, *Conversation, Language, and Possibilities*, 135–36.

"MY SHRINK"

Not-knowing is most fully expressed in its curious questions. How do you know what questions to ask? I learned that the client's answer to one question told me what I needed to ask next. This story is a case in point: Andrew was failing middle school, although he was highly intelligent. In elementary school, he made As and Bs but then his grades began to fall. Even when he did his homework, he would forget to take it to school or he would bury it in the bottom of his book bag. He suffered from depression, anxiety, and guilt about his poor grades. His parents asked me to see him, and for different periods I was his pastoral counselor from the time he was in middle school into his first year of college. He referred to me as "My Shrink."

Andrew did well in the classroom, and he made high scores on standardized tests. He even made As in several of his advanced placement classes but Cs and Ds in many others. His repeated failure to participate in activities he considered "busy work," such as turning in his homework, dragged him down academically and emotionally. He excelled in other areas of his life and was elected governor at Boys State.[9] He and his parents feared that he wasn't going to make it through high school and into college. In a session with his parents, they told me how they had tried one thing after another to help Andrew get his schoolwork done with little or no success. These well-educated, high-functioning parents were tormented by their predicament.

Earlier, his father had sent me an angry email saying Andrew had been in therapy with me all this time, and things hadn't changed. Was I doing my job? This is part of a conversation in a session I had with Andrew's mother and father:

---

9. "American Legion Boys State is among the most respected and selective educational programs of government instruction for US high school students. The training centers on the structure of city, county and state governments. Operated by students elected to various offices, Boys State activities include legislative sessions, court proceedings, law-enforcement presentations, assemblies, bands, choruses and recreational programs." American Legion, "American Legion Boys Nation."

Narrative Means to Educational Ends

Father: We're trying hard to help Andrew, but nothing we try has really worked.

Mother: We are at an angry standoff because he resents anything we do to try to help him. In fact, what we try to do to help seems to make things worse.

Father: We can't just give up. What else can we do?

Dick: What do you think would happen if you quit trying to help him?

Mother: I'm afraid it would just get worse.

Dick: How would it get worse?

Father: He will get failing grades.

Dick: What would happen then?

Father: He won't get his high school degree.

Dick: And then what would happen?

Mother: He would not be able to go to college.

Dick: And what would happen if he didn't go to college?

Father: He wouldn't be able to get a good professional job and make a decent living.

Dick: And where would that put you, his parents? (long pause)

Father: You think we should just quit trying?

Dick: What do you think?

Father: Well, what we're doing certainly isn't working.

Dick: If you quit trying, do you think your relationship with Andrew would improve?

Mother: Maybe?

His parents were, in fact, able to stop helping Andrew with his schoolwork. And in doing so they acted with exceptional courage. They told Andrew they were going to leave his schoolwork up to him. They weren't giving up on him, but they were quitting the job of offering incentives and disincentives to help him make good grades. Months later Andrew told me that his relationship with his parents had improved; in fact, he said, it had never been better. Son and parents enjoyed being with each other, and he felt less guilty about his bad grades. It turns out that he did manage to graduate from high school, and he graduated from college, though not with an outstanding GPA. To his parents' surprise, he then applied to law school at American University and was accepted, finished his law degree, and became a practicing attorney.

When I began this conversation with Andrew's parents, I did not know where it would take us. I think my questions and their responses tapped into wisdom they didn't know they had. In this wisdom, they were able to see a completely unexpected alternative narrative. That narrative said that their relationship with Andrew was more important than his academic success. The problem-saturated story had kept them from seeing and enacting what they deeply believed.

I had a conversation with Andrew's parents some eleven years after they'd stopped trying to help him with his school work. Of that decision, his father said, "The most important effect has been our relationship with our children. Andrew and Allen [Andrew's brother] actually seem to like us and want to spend time with us! They see a stark contrast between their friends' relationships with their parents and their relationship with us." He went on to say, "I do not exaggerate in saying we tell the story at least once a month of our son the lawyer who almost flunked out of high school, but with whom we have the warmest and most loving of relationships because of a choice his counselor gave us permission to make."

How did I give them permission to make their courageous decision? I didn't. I asked curious questions, and they gave themselves that permission. From a theological point of view, I believe God influenced their ability to change course with Andrew by God calling them forward to a more vital involvement with their son—an involvement different than trying to help him make good grades. God lured them into a new and unexpected narrative that led them to more intimate and fulfilling relationships with both of their sons.[10]

---

10. See Cobb, *Jesus' Abba*, 100.

The problem-saturated story troubling Andrew and his parents was loaded with conventional cultural wisdom, a discourse that said academic success was the golden key to unlock the future. It was, therefore, completely unacceptable for a bright young man like Andrew to fail academically. Andrew, his parents, and his teachers were locked into this conventional discourse so that it was unthinkable for his parents to quit trying to help Andrew succeed in school. It was unthinkable until the parents courageously broke the lock on this cultural narrative and wrote an alternative story.

CHALLENGING A PATERNALISTIC DISCOURSE BY "ORGANIZING WITH MY HEART"

What follows is another story of a person caught in a set of oppressive cultural expectations. Every day women must deal with the discourse that says that the man's way of doing things is the right way, the preferred way, the acceptable and approved way. This is an account of my narrative work with a woman who dealt with this discourse in her role as an associate minister.

During most of my therapy practice I wrote up notes on a counseling session after the client had left. However, narrative therapy led me to an alternative practice of collaborative documentation with the client. At the end of each session I invited the client, or clients, to sit beside me while I typed up on my laptop the main points of our conversation. I usually opened with the question, "What do you want to remember about our conversation today?" Clients would then reflect with me on the session and from time to time I would ask another curious question. I would type notes of our conversation, then I would print out and give the client a copy of our notes.

Elizabeth, an associate minister in her congregation, made particularly good use of collaborative documentation. At the end of her sessions, she was able to distill what she had learned—learning that came out of her own wisdom. The following account is from our end-of-hour collaborative notes about our sessions.

Her senior pastor had told her that she wasn't a good organizer, and she needed to learn how to do it. She accepted his view of her as disorganized. Worried, she didn't know what to do about his admonition. She made an appointment to see me to deal with her disorganization.

In my first session with her, I learned that she had mystical experiences in which she felt a strong sense of God's presence. She said these experiences with God "are so vibrant they are mystifying to other people and I don't feel comfortable telling those stories." I was struck by the power of these mystical experiences and how they were so different than the norm of her denominational culture that she didn't feel comfortable telling anyone else about them. Yet, they were a clue to how, in fact, she did organize.

In my questions I sought to learn about her way of organizing and not about what the senior minister expected of her. She said, "listening to and collaborating with other people is a way of organizing work. It's just the way I am organizing. Who knew!—that approaching a situation from a not-knowing perspective is not a weakness; it is actually a powerful position." She described how she organized the new confirmation team. "I came with a tentative plan but I held it loosely until I discovered what other people felt strongly about doing. And I gave them equal access to the organizing and let them do what they were good at and what I'm not good at."

She began to bring color in to the organization of her office. She replaced the plain manila folders with folders that had colored designs. "The way that I organize," she said, "has something to do with my heart. I think I have been trying to organize with my head only, and when I started thinking about the colors of the folders and being surrounded by beauty and making time for God—that's making room for my heart—that's organizing using my heart and my head." I asked, "Earlier were you trying to organize without taking your heart into account?" She said, "Yes, but I didn't know it was a possibility. None of the organizational books talk about organizing with your heart. Divinity school sucked my heart dry. It was not for my heart."

While she was seeing me, a sixteen-year-old boy in her congregation died from cancer. She wondered how she would minister to the family and how she would conduct a funeral in this tragic situation. She was quite apprehensive about it. During the week of preparation for the funeral, however, this changed as she listened to her heart. Reflecting on the funeral service later, she said,

> I *can* organize. I organize better when I can work off of my own instincts. We've talked about organizing with my heart and creating a thing of beauty. I think that's why the funeral worked so well. I created a thing of beauty and it came from my heart. It was an act of love. After the service the father said, "Elizabeth, I heard exactly what I needed today." I said, "Good, I needed to hear that it was what you needed."

Toward the end of our ten sessions she said, "I am learning to own my own organizational style, that it's collaborative, needs to be beautiful, and that I organize with my heart. Part of the definition of organizing with your heart is that it's somewhat undefined."

Elizabeth, following her own wisdom, worked her way out of an institutional pattern that was separating head from heart. She found an alternative narrative for herself outside of the conventional, hierarchical, male-dominated denominational culture. When she performed the funeral for a sixteen-year-old boy, this narrative came to full expression.

Although her denomination has made progress in opening up opportunities for female ministers, this story lets us know that male bias continues to exert its influence. Her senior minister was, no doubt, following the norms of the denomination—norms for organization that were developed by men. These male norms were getting in the way of Elizabeth organizing with her heart.

NARRATIVE THERAPY AS EDUCATION

Narrative therapy, as evident in my experiences with Andrew and Elizabeth, is more than therapy. It is educational. The Latin term *educare* means "to lead out," "to draw out," and "to bring forth." In narrative therapy, this root meaning of education describes a process of bringing forth from clients their own knowledge and understanding. A narrative therapy approach enabled Andrew's parents and Elizabeth to identify and appreciate their own untapped wisdom. It was not my wisdom as their therapist. My work was to relate to them in a way that made it possible for them to be educated by their own knowledge and understanding.

DEVELOPMENT OF THE NARRATIVE THERAPY SEMINAR

In 1996, I left my job in Atlanta to return to Raleigh where I rejoined the staff of Triangle Pastoral Counseling (TPC). I had done counseling there one day a week while I taught at Southeastern Seminary (1975–91). A year after I returned to the TPC staff, I offered a narrative therapy seminar for therapists, and I led this seminar for fifteen years, from 1997 to 2012, until Beverly and I moved to Matthews, near Charlotte. The seminar has continued, facilitated by Jack McKinney, and at this writing in 2024 it is in its twenty-seventh year.

The narrative therapy seminar has continued for more than a quarter century. What has sustained its vitality and longevity? I believe that these aspects have kept it going as a vital educational venture.

Three-Hour Sessions That Meet Twice a Month in Six- to Nine-Month "Terms" or Semesters

Participants sign up to be present for a defined period of time. Meeting in "terms" heightens membership commitment and gives the participants the option to enroll in the seminar for a term and then decide whether to sign up for the next term. The expectation is that if you signed up for a term you will be present at each session.

Covenant or Ground Rules

Each term, the participants consider, revise, and commit to follow a covenant (often called *ground rules*):

1. Stay curious and observe the rule from Parker Palmer: No fixing, no saving, no advising, no setting anyone straight.
2. Protect the confidentiality of each person by promising not to share what anyone says in our meetings outside these meetings unless they give us permission to do so.
3. Observe time limits.
4. If you must be absent, let us know ahead of time.

Group Facilitation for the Three-Hour Session

Responsibilities for facilitating each session are rotated among the six to nine participants. The facilitator sees that the seminar begins and ends on time and that each segment of the session stays within its time boundaries. This firm structure might appear to be constraining. Actually it diminishes anxiety in the group and gives people a sense of freedom knowing that the facilitator will manage the time effectively, and they don't have to worry about it. For example, "I don't have to be anxious that I won't have enough time to present my case."

Segments of Seminar Sessions

The segments of each seminar session are: poetry, the question for the day, connecting the assigned readings, a break, a case presentation using a reflecting team, and a time to reflect on the entire session. The specified times are in parentheses.

Theological Education in a New Key

Poetry Using Lectio Divina

Lectio divina is a monastic practice for reading scripture—particularly in the Benedictine Order. The seminar does this practice with poetry instead of scripture. As with other parts of the agenda, participants take their turn to bring in a poem. The poem is read three times, each time by a different person, with a pause between readings. The poem provides participants a transition into liminal space as they leave their work-a-day world to join each other across a threshold into a different way of belonging. Here is one of my poems. (9:15–9:35)

AT EASE IN ZION

In 1960 Baylor University was
an all-white school in
segregated central Texas.

I was taking history from
Rufus Spain who was troubled by
this pervasive racist culture.

He told this story. He was waiting
at a bus stop, standing beside
an African American woman.

He asked the class, "When the bus
stopped, who do you think got on
first? The Negro woman or me?"

He paused while the question
sunk in. Then he said, "I got on first."

He was struggling against racism
in himself, and he confessed how
his prejudice won out
at that bus stop.

Spain's personal story has stayed
with me because in that traditional
class setting, in that moment,
in that segregated university,
he let us see the inner world
of his own prejudice.

His story was an invitation for us
to examine the prejudice every one
of us carried within ourselves.[11]

Question for the Day

A member is responsible for bringing a question that engages the participants at a personal level. The question grows out of the poem. From this poem one could draw a question such as: What story do you have in which you realized your prejudice won out over your better self? (9:35–10:15)

The Challenge to Find Connections
Between the Two Readings for the Day

The seminar worked with two assigned textbooks—one from narrative therapy and another from theology. Readings from each text were scheduled side by side with no attempt to see that they were correlated with each other. The member who is responsible for leading the discussion of the readings for the day facilitates the participants figuring out how the two texts could speak to each other. (10:15–10:50)

---

11. Spain continued to work on racism in himself and in his denomination, and in 1967 he published *At Ease in Zion* about the failure of Southern Baptists, in the aftermath of the Civil War, to challenge the racism that terrorized African Americans and forever stained American history with their blood. Spain, *At Ease in Zion*.

Break

One of the rotated group assignments may be to bring refreshments for the break. (10:50–11:00)

Case Presentation Using a Reflecting Team

The case presentation takes an hour. The presenter's case may be of a client or of some personal issue. (11:00–12:00)

- The presenter chooses a listener and talks only to the listener. (20 minutes)
- After the presentation, the group observes a time of silence. (1 minute)
- The rest of the group comprises a reflecting team. Members of the reflecting team have not spoken to the presenter or listener. The reflecting team members talk among themselves about what they've overheard, and the presenter and listener overhear this conversation. (15 minutes)
- The presenter responds to what has been overheard from the reflecting team, helped by the listener who keeps the focus on what the reflecting team has said. Presenter and listener speak only to each other. The reflecting team remains silent. (10 minutes)
- The boundary between the reflecting team and the presenter-listener dyad is removed and everyone joins the conversation. (15 minutes)

Reflecting Team Members Follow This Guidance

Talk to each other about what you have overheard, and ask each other questions about what the presenter has said. Build on one another's ideas. Keep your responses brief because the presenter can only absorb a limited number of thoughts. Don't give advice, evaluate, analyze, or try to plant your ideas in the presenter's mind. Follow the countercultural rule Parker Palmer uses with his Circles of Trust: "No fixing, no saving, no advising, no setting each other straight."[12] The reflecting team process offers the possibility for presenters, overhearing the team's conversation, to hear things that do not fit the problem story. This opens the way for the presenter to discover alternative narratives to the problem-saturated one that's been closing off other possibilities.[13] Reflecting team members remain curious, and they exercise a relentless optimism about the presenter and the problem. Because this practice deviates so radically from conventional wisdom, conventional conversations, and conventional therapy case presentations, reflecting team members often struggle to do it.

Reflect on the Session

Participants look back on the entire three-hour session and talk about what has stood out for them; what linked different parts together? Was the reflecting team able to refrain from giving advice? What part has the poem played during the session? What would the participants want to do differently in future sessions? (12:00–12:15)

Engage in a Relentless Optimism

Relentless optimism is based on the conviction that the problem story is never the whole story. This optimism does not ignore the negative power of the problem story and the ways the presenter may feel trapped. But the problem can be *externalized* and separated from the person. Then one can ask about it in personalized form—What gives it power? What takes its power away? What is it trying to do to its owner? This optimistic stance takes the negative power of the problem story fully into account, but it looks for exceptions to that story. Elizabeth was struggling with her belief that she did not know how to organize. As she told about her work she recalled how she had organized the confirmation class in an open-ended way and that

---

12. Palmer, *Hidden Wholeness*, 114.
13. Andersen, *Reflecting Team*, 16.

it worked for her and the lay leaders involved—an exception to the problem story that said she couldn't get organized.

Relentless optimism as practiced in the narrative therapy seminar is grounded in the belief that God is constantly at work in our personal and collective stories to realize what Desmond Tutu has called "God's dream."[14] Although we may not be aware of it, I believe God's persistent, compassionate presence is there nonetheless. However, unless this presence is storied, it goes undetected. The reflecting team is in a position to notice evidence that may point to God's presence which the presenter hasn't been able to see.

David Verner tells how the reflecting team approach affected him personally as well as professionally.

> The most powerful piece of the seminar is the reflecting team with the attitude that we're listening with curiosity and also with optimism about the work. It's listening for the strength, listening for what is generative. If there's some issue that seems to be undermining, then we'll take a look at that, but it's not where we start. This approach had such positive repercussions for me on so many levels—in relationships with colleagues, with clients, with myself, my family—that's really revolutionary.

Influence of the Narrative Therapy Seminar on the Culture of the Counseling Center

From its early years, the center employed Alan Carter, MD, as a psychiatric consultant who signed off on insurance claims and led the weekly case conference. During his long tenure, Alan became a valued adjunctive member of the staff. He led case conferences from a medical psychiatric perspective, and he led with wit and wisdom. He also had the final word on diagnoses and on the quality of counselors' work with their clients. In 2001, Alan resigned as our medical consultant due to the increased cost of liability insurance for providing this service.

---

14. Tutu, *God Has a Dream*.

In the void that followed upon Alan's resignation, I asked to present a case using the reflecting team model being practiced in the narrative therapy seminar. After that, other members of the staff also began to ask for the reflecting team when they presented their cases. After a while the reflecting team process became the established practice in our weekly case conferences.

The norms of the reflecting team model have had a positive effect on the culture of the center. Staff members have been more willing to take a not-knowing position toward a problem or a proposal. Leadership has become more egalitarian, with the director trusting the staff to shape the direction of the organization. Staff meetings are led not by the director but by a facilitator from among the staff. This role is rotated among staff members in three-month terms. Competition among staff members, while always present, has been tempered by the not-knowing outlook. Staff members began to take a more hopeful view of the center's future, and the half-empty glass more often became half-full.

Exporting the Narrative Therapy Seminar Model

Suzanne Luper was the director of Triangle Pastoral Counseling when I started the narrative therapy seminar. The center is a member of the Samaritan Institute,[15] a national organization of pastoral counseling centers. Suzanne was invited to join a leadership consultation group for Samaritan center directors. When they met together, center directors brought in cases of leadership issues in their center. Each director had a group session in which to present an issue. Suzanne reported that "members of this group had a reputation of being *the* elite, hot group of master therapists. And they were good. They were also very competitive and often got so excited about their own ideas that they were all talking at one time." For three years Suzanne experienced the tension between her experience in this group and her experience at Triangle Pastoral Counseling where case presentations followed the model adopted from the narrative therapy seminar. Finally, she

15. The Samaritan Institute is now the Solihten Institute.

asked if she could present her case using that model instead of the unstructured model the group usually followed. She said,

> I had written out the time allotments, and I gave a brief explanation of what the roles were. And the huge difference was that I didn't talk to the group, I talked to a listener. And the rest of the therapists could not interrupt me. The reflecting team conversation of the other therapists followed. It was radically different, and I was able to talk about the energy that I did not have to use for anticipating questions and defending myself or trying to explain myself.

When she talked with the group of therapists about how she had presented her case in this different way, she said, "I could hear one idea at a time, and I did not have to respond, just take it in, take what I can use and let the rest go."

She reported that "doing the case this narrative way brought about a real change in that group, and from that point on people basically said, 'I want what she had!'" The change wasn't sudden but gradually more members began asking to present their case this way until it became "the standard fare." "And what it did in that group was to reduce the amount of competitiveness from a 10 to a 2. It was huge. Which, I think, in turn, increased our intimacy. I was in the group for ten years, and we have a reunion now every five years."

By asking to use a reflecting team to present her case, Suzanne began to lay bare the secret that competition was undermining the group's purpose, which was to provide mutual support and wisdom.

Kelli Walker-Jones succeeded Suzanne as the center's director, and she also joined a Samaritan Institute directors' support group. She tells how she introduced the reflecting team in her group:

> The very first leadership group meeting I went to I asked if I could do my case in a way that was most comfortable to me—out of our tradition at Triangle Pastoral Counseling. But I wouldn't even have asked for that if I hadn't heard Suzanne's story. It wouldn't even have occurred to me to ask for what would be best for me. I did it in such a way that

Narrative Means to Educational Ends

I wasn't trying to change everything. I was just asking for what is best for me.

WHAT KIND OF EDUCATION IS THIS?

In this chapter I have woven together a narrative approach to therapy and a narrative approach to education. Each approach enriches the other. The narrative therapist engages clients with curious questions and not advice or interpretation. Clients experience a not-knowing companion who asks questions that enable them to draw upon their own untapped reservoir of wisdom. When this happens, they begin to discover alternative narratives that are different than the problem-saturated stories that have them stuck.

On the educational side of narrative practice, the narrative therapy seminar creates a learning environment similar to the student groups I wrote about in chapters 3 and 5. It has the power of belonging. Recall that earlier statement by Willie James Jennings that "theological education must capture its central work—to form us in the art of cultivating belonging."[16]

In the narrative therapy seminar, and in the peer-led groups I have described in previous chapters, belonging creates a liminal space where, for a period of time, the participants become a fictive family. They follow a path of unconventional wisdom that for me is embodied in the life of Jesus of Nazareth—particularly his parables. The seminar seeks to lure participants out of the trance of conventional wisdom as they engage in problem-posing education as opposed to banking education. The seminar provides a time and place for participants to explore their personal narratives—inviting them to examine their view of themselves, their values, prejudices, doubts, hopes, and fears. In this educational process the most important textbook is that inner textbook the participants carry within themselves.

---

16. Jennings, *After Whiteness*, 10.

COLLABORATIVE LEARNING

When I started the narrative therapy seminar, I assumed the role of teacher. I planned it, selected the textbooks, facilitated it, and set aside part of it as my time to teach. Then I gradually moved from being the teacher to being a collaborative learner. Jack McKinney told me how he saw my role changing.

> I was in the seminar the last four years you led it. And the thing I noticed even over that last four years was that you were still leading, still doing some active teaching. Each succeeding year you let go of more and more of that. By the end it was a really different feel.
>
> Dick adds: It took me that long to lay aside the professor's gown or whatever you call it.
>
> Jack continues: It had worked so well for you for so long, why would you want to let it go, you know, but you did. And I thought that was a really lovely transition and brought people into the room in a different way.

This description brings us back to Paulo Freire, whose educational approach I discussed in chapter 4, and how he and his team taught the peasants of Brazil to read. Freire knew the peasants were being oppressed by the language of the educated and socially privileged. Therefore, instead of using that privileged language to teach them how to read, he and his team sought to learn the peasants' idiom. Then the team taught literacy with the peasants' indigenous language. In order to accomplish this complex task, the literacy teams met with small groups of peasants and served not as teachers but as facilitators. It was difficult for an educated literacy specialist to lead such a group without dominating it. Therefore facilitators had to learn how to become teacher-learners in dialogue with other learner-teachers.[17]

In my forty-two-year span of teaching, I moved from being the knowing professor to becoming a teacher-learner. I participated in the narrative therapy seminar just like all the other members. I

---

17. Herzog, *Parables as Subversive Speech*, 20.

rotated through the different seminar roles and did not occupy a space reserved for The Teacher. The teaching task had been transformed as all participants became teacher-learners. Then we renamed the narrative therapy seminar. It became "Collaborative Supervision for Narrative Therapy."

THE KEYS

This chapter explored the relationship of narrative therapy to narrative education. Our *personal narratives* are the substance which connect us to other human beings. The structure of the narrative therapy seminar described in this chapter created a liminal space in which these *personal stories could be invited out and told.*

The key of *diversity* is expressed in the consideration of "normalizing truths" that subjugate us to the global truth claims of those in political power. Whiteness is a central normalizing truth, and it works relentlessly against diversity.

Belonging, being in a fictive family, enables resistance to normalizing truths such as Whiteness. Narrative therapy seeks to resist normalizing truths and adopts a position of not-knowing, which is a fundamental strength of *belonging*—not so much pursuing truth about each other but seeking to understand each other.

QUESTIONS

1. What is the discourse of Whiteness?
2. What is the difference between an interracial perspective and a perspective of Whiteness?
3. Have you tried taking a not-knowing position toward some problem, challenge, or difficulty? How did that work out?
4. What features of the narrative therapy seminar stand out for you? Why are they important to you?

5. What power/knowledge discourses were at work in the two cases discussed in this chapter—the boy who was failing in school and the associate minister who was told she needed to learn how to organize?

8

Know Your Story and Lead with It
The Sustaining Pastoral Excellence Project

WHAT THE NARRATIVE THERAPY seminar taught me and my colleagues during its first six years went into an application I made on behalf of Triangle Pastoral Counseling to the Lilly Endowment for a Sustaining Pastoral Excellence grant in June 2002. The Endowment sent out a request for proposals that addressed the Endowment's question: "How do you *sustain* the work of pastors who already are doing a good job?" The Endowment staff was utterly surprised to receive more than seven hundred proposals. Triangle Pastoral Counseling was among the sixty-three projects that Lilly initially funded. We received a first and then a second grant that together totaled more than one million dollars over a six-year period.

As I began working on that project proposal, I realized I could not lead such a project alone and that I needed a female partner to lead it with me. I enlisted Kelli Walker-Jones, an ordained elder in The United Methodist Church, to join me in directing the project.

Not only was Kelli a pastor, she had also been associate director of field education and admissions at Duke University Divinity School. After our project ended in 2009, Kelli was soon named director of Triangle Pastoral Counseling, and she continued to conduct narrative-based workshops, many of which were funded by the Lilly Endowment.

Our project offered interfaith peer groups of eight or nine clergy. Each group met for two years, during which the participants clarified their personal story, built friendships, explored a narrative perspective, and practiced narrative leadership.

THEORETICAL AND LEADERSHIP PERSPECTIVES DICK AND KELLI BROUGHT TO THE PROJECT

Kelly brought to the project her experience as a leader in Odyssey of the Mind, a program that for more than forty years has taught teams of students—from elementary school through college—how to solve open-ended problems. Odyssey teams have to think creatively, outside of the box, to solve an assigned problem. The facilitator has the challenge to support, clarify, and encourage the process without helping the team figure out how to solve the problem.

This perspective of leadership in Odyssey of the Mind fit well with the perspective of narrative therapy which Dick brought to the project—taking a not-knowing position, not analyzing or prescribing solutions, asking curious questions, and listening for evidence of the wisdom and resourcefulness that the client or student or minister brings to a situation.

THE PROJECT LEADERSHIP TEAM

Kelli and I recruited additional project staff from veterans of the narrative therapy seminar—David Verner, Barbara Mann, and Suzanne Luper. These staff members, along with Kelli and me, provided mentoring for each project participant. Our consultants—first Mahan Siler and later Eunice Holbert—facilitated monthly project staff meetings. All these people, except for Eunice, who joined the project later, were active consultants as we wrote the grant. I am convinced that their contribution helped immeasurably in our getting it.

Know Your Story and Lead with It

A CENTRAL IDEA IN THE PROJECT: NO FIXING

We adopted as a guiding principle for the project Parker Palmer's rule for his Circles of Trust: "No fixing, no saving, no advising, no setting each other straight."[1] This countercultural rule goes against the grain of what congregations generally expect of their ministers and what ministers typically expect of themselves. The call to ministry appears to many to be a call to fix, save, advise, and set people straight. We sought to work against this understanding of the call. We invited our participating clergy toward a leadership that is more curious than certain, more invitational than coercive, and more egalitarian than hierarchical. We encouraged them to take a not-knowing position—to be able, in perplexing situations, to admit to themselves and to acknowledge to others when they don't know what to do next—and to see this acknowledgment as a creative response and not as some kind of failure. The theology behind this not-knowing position holds that God is constantly at work in every situation and that the outcome of any of our efforts belongs to God and not to us.

Taking on responsibility for any problem was ingrained in Gene, who was distressed about the behavior of his associate minister. The associate was making inappropriate references in worship services to matters in his personal life. Gene made repeated efforts to change this behavior but failed in his attempts. Finally he did something that was out of character for him. He gave up. He confessed to the church board that he did not know what to do about the associate's behavior. To his immense relief, the board decided that it would assume responsibility for supervising the associate and took the problem out of his hands.

Months later, Gene thickened this story of not knowing with a story of not fixing. He came upon a group of church members, clustered in the hall, asking each other who was going to put up the Vacation Bible School sign in front of the church. As he approached, they all turned to him—he who had a tool box in his office to take

---

1. Palmer, *Hidden Wholeness*, 114.

care of such things. He surprised them and himself by exchanging pleasantries with them and then walking away. As he turned away he said to himself, "I'm tired of doing things that aren't in my job description." He said that his entire body resisted turning away, producing a knot in the pit of his stomach. Part of him said he should go back and put up the sign. But another part said to him, "No, don't do it. This is your opportunity to not be helpful." He paid attention to this different inner voice, and someone else put up the sign.[2]

MY DISORIENTATION AND REORIENTATION IN THE PROJECT

As we began our work with our first group of clergy, I experienced something similar to what happened to Gene. I found myself disoriented and had to find my way to a new orientation.

I was accustomed to teaching seminary classes. I expected that I would be able to do the same form of teaching in this project. That didn't happen. We were leading groups of full-time ministers of congregations. They did not have the time, energy, or inclination to do work like what I assigned in seminary classes, and I didn't have the leverage of a professor in an academic system. In my seminary classes I had worked hard to create an egalitarian culture, and I was successful to a point. However, the project culture went beyond that. I had to set aside assumptions associated with my power as a professor. I held no grade book and could grant no academic credit. My only leverage was whether the participants believed I was acting in their best interests or not. I knew I was in a different territory than the seminary classroom.

---

2. This story and most of the following stories about project participants in this chapter are drawn from Hester and Walker-Jones, *Know Your Story*, 54–55.

Know Your Story and Lead with It

A SECOND CENTRAL IDEA IN THE PROJECT: THERE'S ALWAYS ANOTHER STORY

The first central idea in the project was "No fixing, no saving, no advising, no setting each other straight." The second central idea in the project was "There's always another story." When we tell a story of an event we're selective. We choose only parts of what actually happened to construct our account because we cannot possibly include everything that occurred. We select, reject, connect, pare, smooth out, lengthen this, compress that. We tidy up a messy conglomeration of information to create a story of what happened, and we usually do this in a few seconds. Consequently much of the information about the event lies about us on the cutting room floor. We've gone on and left these remains behind.

This reality was manifest dramatically when one of our newly formed groups was walking several blocks from our office condo to lunch at a Chinese restaurant. On the way, a preoccupied driver moving slowly out of a driveway struck Wanda, one of our participants. She fell in the street. The group immediately sprang into action. Ed, who was well versed in first aid, went to care for Wanda. Kathy, who was walking right behind Wanda, had banged on the hood of the car to stop the driver. Kelli stepped into the street to direct traffic around Wanda. Someone called the police. Ed found that Wanda had survived without injury, and she rejoined the group.

In a short time, we had dealt with the emergency. Wanda ended up comforting the distraught woman driver. We continued our trip to the restaurant.

When we reconvened after lunch, Kelli and I asked that each person take a turn to tell what happened on our way to the Chinese restaurant. And we got eleven different versions of the event. It was an unplanned lesson that memorably demonstrated for us all that there's always another story about anything that happens. Any story we tell is only one version of the event, and we can never gather up all the pieces and tell the whole story.[3]

---

3. Hester and Walker-Jones, *Know Your Story*, 9–10.

One of our participants, Sally, got fed up with her congregation's board meetings that were filled with complaints. Certain board members held a dark view that the church was in serious trouble, and they expected the minister to do something about it. As one board meeting spiraled down into the usual fog of criticism and predictions of congregational decline, she said, "I want to ask you to stop this conversation and imagine me locking the doors to this room. And I'm not going to unlock them until I hear you talk about the strengths you see in our church." The gloomy story of the church stalled, then stopped. Finally, one person thought of a positive piece of congregational life. Then someone else told of another strength. Gradually the atmosphere in the room began to change as the pace of positive statements picked up. Before long, they had put together an entirely unexpected affirming story that stood over against the pessimistic narrative. Things were not all bright and rosy, but the minister had succeeded in closing the door on a gloomy narrative that for months had been infecting board meetings. She did this because she understood that there's always another story, and she devised a creative intervention to help board members explore and find this other, more positive, story about the congregation.

THERE'S ALWAYS ANOTHER STORY: CASTE AND RACE

In her book on caste in the US, Isabel Wilkerson contends that in America the alternative narrative to every other narrative we tell or write is the narrative of caste and race. Although we couldn't see it at the time, this was the case in our project. Wilkerson writes that

> America has an unseen skeleton, a caste system that is as central to its operation as are the studs and joists that we cannot see in the physical buildings we call home. Caste is the infrastructure of our divisions. It is the architecture of human hierarchy, the subconscious code of instructions for maintaining, in our case, a four-hundred-year-old social order.... If we have been trained to see humans in the language of race, then caste is the underlying grammar that we encode as children, as when learning our mother tongue.

> Caste, like grammar, becomes an invisible guide not only to how we speak, but to how we process information, the autonomic calculations that figure into a sentence without our having to think about it.[4]

Caste and race were not a part of our proposal for this project, and we did not make it an explicit part of the project agenda. Caste and race were nonetheless present, and they qualified all we did in the more than six years of the project, although we were not aware of it. One participant, however, made the issue of race visible because she was a person of color.

Dorothy was a minister in the Metropolitan Community Church (MCC). She was the only Black person in our Sustaining Pastoral Excellence Project. I called her in April 2021, to ask her to tell me about her experience in the project. At the time of the project, she was pastor of an MCC congregation. When we talked she held an administrative position in the MCC denomination.

I asked Dorothy what it was like to be the only Black person in the SPE group. "I didn't really feel a part and felt that at times the group did not understand me as a person of color and a lesbian," she said. "I expected to see other people of color in the program and was surprised to find out that I was the only one and shocked when you told me that I was the only one in the whole project."

She said the hardest part of her participation was doing the family genograms. "I did not know very much about my family history. I got questions like, 'Why don't you know more?' Other group members presented 'wholesome' families, and this was something I was unfamiliar with. I felt ashamed."

"The closest I felt to the group was the day-long retreat when we did the art project. That took us out of the office and into a home-like setting." Art therapist Sue Etheridge led that project, which involved individual art work and then a cooperative, collective creation that called for arranging pieces of our different individual art together into a collage. "I felt more engagement that day," Dorothy recalled.

---

4. Wilkerson, *Caste*, 17–18.

"Being with the group for the whole day made a difference. Working on the art together seemed to transcend some of our differences."

Dorothy said further, "If I were in the Sustaining Pastoral Excellence group now I would be more vocal. I would look at it differently. I would be more assertive—more in your face. It's a different atmosphere now with Black Lives Matter standing out."

Dorothy was a minority of one in two ways. She was the only Black person in the group, and she was the only openly homosexual person in the group. Her identity was an issue to which we, as the project directors, needed to give our attention. How wise was it for us to have enlisted only one Black person in the group? Did she not need companions of color there with her? She was leading an LGBTQ congregation of African American women. Was her congregation an untapped resource for our SPE group? What would have happened if we had invited her to arrange for our group to meet with members of her congregation? What would we straight, White people have learned?

RECOGNIZING COLORBLIND RACISM AND WHITE FRAGILITY

What prevented us project directors, and the participants in Dorothy's group, from recognizing and acknowledging Dorothy's distinctive presence in the group as an African American? It may be the case that all of us were under the spell of colorblind racism. Ben Boswell describes this phenomenon:

> In 2008, conservative and liberal commentators celebrated the election of Barack Obama as the first black president of the United States as the sign that America had become a "post-racial" society.... Polls, however, indicated that white Americans were far more likely than black Americans to believe they were living in a post-racial society.
>
> The idea of a "post-racial" society was consistent with the beliefs that a majority of white Americans held for over a decade: i.e. that African Americans had achieved, or would soon achieve, racial equality in the United States despite

substantial evidence to the contrary. Eduardo Bonilla-Silva states, "The white commonsense view on racial matters is that racists are few and far between, discrimination has all but disappeared since the 1960s, and most whites are color blind . . . [and] whites seem to be collectively shouting, 'We have a black president, so we are finally beyond race.'"[5]

Declaring Obama's election to be the advent of a "post-racial" society was both a form of false optimism and denial about the problem of race, which not only proved to be untrue, but performed a re-branding of the insidious myth of colorblind racism.[6]

Colorblind racism is frequently reinforced by White fragility. Critical discourse scholar Robin DiAngelo defines White fragility as "a state in which even a minimum amount of racial stress becomes intolerable, triggering a range of defensive moves. These moves include the outward display of emotions such as anger, fear, and guilt, and behaviors such as argumentation, silence, and leaving the stress-inducing situation."[7]

Boswell observes that colorblind racism together with White fragility inhibit racial dialogue because these conditions lead White people to engage in conversations about race as if race is a problem for people of color and not something they must face within themselves.[8]

Having named the alternative narrative of caste and race and its almost hidden presence, I turn now to explore the explicit and conscious narrative of the project.

STRATEGIES THAT HELPED PARTICIPANTS EXPLORE THEIR OWN STORIES

Our Sustaining Pastoral Excellence Project did not teach pastors how to improve their ministry. Rather, we used different strategies to help

---

5. Bonilla-Silva, *Racism Without Racists*, 25.
6. Boswell, "Identifying Whiteness," 8–9.
7. Boswell, "Identifying Whiteness," 3–4, paraphrasing DiAngelo, *White Fragility*.
8. Boswell, "Identifying Whiteness," 4–5.

them investigate their own stories. In so doing, we enabled them to use the wisdom they already carried within themselves to exercise creative leadership such as that described in the stories above. This is what Kelli had to say about it: "Most of my vocation has been in the context of the congregation or seminary staff. In both places there was always conversation about one more thing that clergy could do to become more effective. I became allergic to any advice or practice that promised to improve my work—the assumption being that my work was never good enough." She went on to say that in this project, "No one was telling these clergy, 'Here's what you need to do to improve your work.'" Instead, we used strategies to help the members of our clergy groups get in touch with the resources available to them within their own stories. We sought to help them open and explore their inner textbooks. *The strategies we employed included these.*

Hospitality

In chapter 6, I explored the creation of liminal space in small student groups. In this project we worked to create liminal space with our hospitality. The focus of hospitality in these groups was the enjoyment of a generous meal together provided by a nearby restaurant. Years later Dorothy reflected on the hospitality of the group and said, "It was a place to take time for myself. It was a respite. It allowed me to be removed from the work of ministry for four hours twice a month. You provided everything—the structure, the food, everything. I still talk about the group."

Lectio Divina and Poetry

Following the model of the narrative therapy seminar discussed in chapter 7, we began each of our sessions with poetry following the monastic practice of *lectio divina*—reading the poem three times with pauses between each reading and then inviting reflections on it. A poem that expressed the difficulty clergy face in caring for a congregation was "The Journey" by Mary Oliver. On the one hand, it expresses the daunting challenge of pastoral leadership, and on the other hand it describes the freedom of not capitulating to oppressive leadership demands.

> One day you finally knew
> what you had to do, and began,
> though the voices around you
> kept shouting
> their bad advice—
> though the whole house
> began to tremble
> and you felt the old tug
> at your ankles.
> "Mend my life!"
> each voice cried.
> But you didn't stop.
> You knew what you had to do,
> though the wind pried
> with its stiff fingers
> at the very foundations,
> though their melancholy
> was terrible.
> It was already late
> enough, and a wild night,
> and the road full of fallen
> branches and stones.
> But little by little,
> as you left their voices behind,
> the stars began to burn
> through the sheets of clouds
> and there was a new voice
> which you slowly
> recognized as your own,
> that kept you company
> as you strode deeper and deeper
> into the world,
> determined to do
> the only thing you could do—
> determined to save
> the only life you could save.[9]

---

9. Oliver, *New and Selected Poems*, 114–15.

Theological Education in a New Key

Early Childhood Memories and Biblical Stories

We asked our participants to tell one of their earliest childhood memories and how they would relate that memory to their work as a minister. Sandra is a fifty-one-year-old minister who complained about hitting the glass ceiling in her denominational system. She told an early childhood memory of being on a small airliner, seated next to the window with her mother on the aisle seat holding her baby brother. She wiggled free and went running down the aisle, her mother unable to stop her because she was holding the baby. Only a curtain separated the pilots from the passengers, and she swept past it and into the cockpit. She saw the pilots and the control panel. No sooner had she made her entrance than a flight attendant picked her up and returned her to her mother, who then prevented further escapes.

Sandra felt she was being held back by the denominational system and described herself as "The Queen of Ain't It Awful" because of her habit of complaining about her situation. Her early memory was a picture of her feeling caught in a system that gave men a privileged edge over women. In the group she was asked whether her story perhaps could be divided into two narratives—one of being held back but another one of breaking free and successfully entering the pilot's domain. She then reported that in her present appointment the congregation had just given her a favorable evaluation. She was so grateful for this evaluation that she wanted "to frame it." Her gratitude was an alternative story to being "The Queen of Ain't It Awful."

In a conversation with her mentor, Sandra related her early memory to the story of Moses who led the people through the desert but who wasn't allowed to enter the promised land. It spoke to her experience of being held back but it also helped her identify with a strong leader. Moreover, she saw that Moses led the people for forty years and that she, like Moses, will have served for forty years when she ends her ministry. "I want people to say I was faithful," she said, "faithful to serve God in small churches wherever I was called. I didn't get to be pastor of a big church, but it doesn't matter. Faithfulness is what matters. If they can say that, I'll have been a success."[10]

Tell a Story of Being a Leader Before You Were Twenty

The memory of leadership before twenty is an exercise similar to the early childhood memory work. It gave the participants a way to gather from the past an account that could help them understand their present leadership. In high school, Ed's swimming coach wanted him to replace another member of the swim relay team after the team had already qualified for a swim meet. Ed thought it wasn't right for him to replace a team member who had already qualified for the team. And he didn't join the team. He continued to challenge superiors during his ministry career. He became a mentor to other clergy and often took the initiative to care for ministers who were having difficulty—championing their welfare when no one else did. Although he faced considerable resistance, he got the denomination to provide care for a minister who suffered a disabling emotional illness.[11]

Case Presentations

In each meeting one participant presented a case, telling about a leadership issue they faced. We used the case presentation model developed in the narrative therapy seminar and outlined in chapter 7.

The most challenging part of these case presentations was following the "no fixing, no saving, no advising, no setting each other straight" rule because it runs so counter to the typical cultural pattern of hearing someone express a problem and wanting to respond by fixing it. The listening partner and the reflecting team often had a hard time holding in check their temptation to offer advice. The project directors, I must add, also had a hard time holding their advice in check.

---

10. Hester and Walker-Jones, *Know Your Story*, 26–28.
11. Hester and Walker-Jones, *Know Your Story*, 31.

Will describes what happened when the group succeeded in taking a not-knowing position in these case presentations:

> We often entered the "unknown" of our lives and the lives of others in the group without judging, without advising, and without solving. The ministry of presence to one another, of walking together in the darkness, seemed to bring light into the abyss of the unknown. Such an experience speaks volumes to me as a pastor about the multitude of abysses we enter. No pastor can have the answer to every problem that comes up. The greater realization is that I don't *have* to have the answer, but I do need to be present and faithful as I walk with my members through their "unknowns."[12]

Creating a Poem out of Paragraphs from an Interview

The project mentors interviewed participants about their life in ministry. The interviews were recorded and transcribed so that group members got a hard copy of their interview. We then invited them to create a poem by taking a block of their interview and removing words until they have a poem, a process known as "erasure poetry." In her interview Kay talked about how her brother's mental illness and his death influenced the way she understood her ministry. This is part of her interview.

> While I was in seminary, you know, my brother died and he was living in an urban area, and he sometimes was homeless, 'cause sometimes he would kind of lose his way, because he suffered from a severe form of schizophrenia (pause) and so I think, this kind of, you know, living in San Francisco and (pause) and being one of those people that's challenged and kind of gets lost in the system, in the city (pause), and he died while I was in seminary, and (pause) so that's one of my, you know, my convergences. I mean, I think, you know, being involved in outreach ministry as mission was always there, because it was such a big focus in the conservative churches I grew up in, but the more social justice, kind of

12. Hester and Walker-Jones, *Know Your Story*, 38.

broader awareness to the world's way of looking at it, that I felt over time, also intersected with my brother's lost place in the world (pause), and so when I wrote my dissertation, you know, I, I did speak to him.

Here is a part of the poem that Kay created by removing words from this block of her interview. She did not change words or their order.

WHILE I WAS IN SEMINARY

My brother died.
Homeless,
sometimes he would lose his way,
suffered schizophrenia,
living in San Francisco,
lost in the system,
in the city,
he died.

Convergence.
Mission, outreach,
churches I grew up in,
social justice,
broader awareness,
intersected
my brother's lost place in the world.

My dissertation.
I did speak to him . . .

The interview text and the poem are longer than the excerpts printed here. Her poem ends with this stanza:

God's presence in suffering.
Always,
always the plea
take care of the homeless
in your midst,
because you were once homeless,

wandering,
God in the exile.[13]

When we asked Kay for permission to include her paragraph and poem in our earlier book, she had not read the poem in months. "I had forgotten how powerful it is," she told us after re-reading it. The poem draws out of the interview the power that otherwise remains untapped in its prose.

Mentoring

Kay's poem came from her sessions with her mentor. She and the other participants in our project met each month with a mentor from the Triangle Pastoral Counseling staff—including Kelli and me. This gave us a chance for more intimate one-on-one conversations with each participant than was possible in the group setting.

The following story tells how Ben used his relationship with his mentor to survive a disastrous annual evaluation of the pastor and staff. Ben was a seasoned and successful clergy leader who, during two years in our project, was pastor of the fastest growing congregation in his denomination in the state. The chair of the committee responsible for staff evaluations was a real estate agent who used a performance review instrument out of the real estate industry.

The evaluation Ben received for his work as senior minister amounted to a slap in the face. It thoroughly repudiated his leadership and recommended that he get a "mini-MBA" in order to become an effective leader. This evaluation disoriented him and sent him into despair. After he had shared this story with his mentor, the mentor said, "I think this evaluation is dead wrong. Would it help for me to write up my thoughts about it?" Ben welcomed this. The mentor wrote that the evaluation appeared to be one person's opinion and not the work of the committee and that it provided no supporting evidence for its unfounded conclusions. The mentor consulted the denomination's prescribed method for evaluating a senior

---

13. Hester and Walker-Jones, *Know Your Story*, 38–40.

minister and staff members, and he wrote that the evaluations Ben and his staff received had utterly no relationship to the denomination's required procedure. The mentor's email opened up an entirely different narrative that countered the negative evaluation Ben had received and affirmed his effectiveness as a spiritual leader. "I was in a boat, lost out in the ocean," he said to the mentor, "then I heard a rescue plane, and that plane was you." This highly successful pastor, reflecting on his overall experience in his group, later acknowledged, "I wouldn't be in the ministry today if it were not for this project."

It appears that in this case the mentor set aside the project norm of *not fixing* in response to Ben's distressed response over his evaluation. Ben expressed immense relief and gratitude for the mentor's intervention. But how could the mentor have responded in a supportive way without helping? The mentor might have asked, "Do you feel that this evaluation is off target, wrong, misguided?" If Ben had said, "Yes" that would have given him a direction to deal with the misguided evaluation. The mentor could simply have asked, "What would the denominational manual tell you about the prescribed procedure for the minister's annual evaluation?" That would have been sufficient to lead Ben to take charge of the problem-solving process rather than it being in the hands of the mentor.

I was, in fact, the mentor in this situation. And I was quite satisfied with my response. Upon reflection, however, I now see that I failed to hold to the norm of *not fixing*. In situations like this it's difficult for me to look for a non-fixing alternative narrative.

Ben presented his evaluation experience as a case for his project group—confessing how vulnerable he felt and how, in his despair, he thought his ministry was a failure. Others who looked upon him as the most successful pastor in the group were relieved to know that even he had doubts and struggles like theirs. His case presentation took the group to a deeper level of trust and intimacy.

Drawing and Presenting Genograms That Pictured One's Family History

A genogram is a family tree that goes back several generations.[14] We invited our clergy participants to draw their genogram, their family tree, as it unfolded over three generations—back to their parents, their grandparents, and their great grandparents—including the children of these relationships, their spouses, and their children. A person constructing the genogram could be as spare or as extensive as they wanted to be. The genogram had symbols to indicate divorces, remarriages, conflicts, emotional cut-offs, mental illness, etc. The genogram gave participants a way to see how family members in past generations had contributed to their present personal and professional story.

Participants drew their genograms on a sheet of newsprint. They were given about an hour to draw this family tree. Then we invited them to present their genogram to the group, describing key relationships and events and the influence of these events on their present life and ministry.

Sharon had presented her genogram to the group and invited responses. Well into these responses someone said, "It looks like in each generation there are emotional cut-offs—people who stop relating to some other person or some other part of the family. I wonder what you make of that?" Sharon was silent as she looked at her genogram and at these cut-offs. She said, "I had never thought about these cut-offs, but there they are. I'm kind of stunned to see them."

I discovered the power of genograms when I did my own genogram and then had conversations with members of my family about it. Several months after my father's death, I showed his two sisters, Gerry Gary and Lottie Means, my genogram of our family. In the midst of this conversation, they told me this story. Their father, my paternal grandfather, John Hester, owned a variety store in their town, Goldthwaite, Texas, and had stocked it heavily for the Christmas season in December 1930. That month, a winter storm struck

---

14. McGoldrick et al., *Genogram*.

and buried the town in an unprecedented blanket of snow. No one could get to town. Left with a store full of merchandise and no sales, John went broke. At the same time John's oldest daughter, Gerry, my aunt, suffered a ruptured appendix. Penicillin hadn't yet been developed. Without it, she spent weeks with her mother by her side in the Brownwood, Texas, hospital near death. According to my aunts, John "went slightly nuts" as he faced this financial disaster and his daughter about to die.

When he learned of the family crisis, my father left his studies at Southern Methodist University to come home to help the family—never to return to college. He got a job with the Texas Highway Department surveying a new highway between Goldthwaite and Brownwood. Then in 1936 he was hired as an operator for the little Goldthwaite power plant, beginning his career as a self-taught electrical engineer.

Without the genogram and this visit with my aunts, I would never have known how my father left college to come to the rescue of the family, nor would I have known how he began his career as an electrical engineer. The genogram drew this story out and made it visible.

LEARNING FROM OUR PARTICIPANTS AND PUBLISHING WHAT WE LEARNED

We were educated by our participants as they dealt with thorny congregational issues. We could see how being a pastor was an impossible job that these participants did nonetheless. Kelli and I witnessed the suffering and the successes of these ministers. And we saw them discover alternative narratives to those that had them mired down.

Our project involved fewer than forty clergy—a far smaller group than most other Sustaining Pastoral Excellence projects. Why was the Lilly Endowment willing to invest in ours? Craig Dykstra, at that time vice president for religion at the Endowment, told Kelli and me that he supported our project because we were developing "intellectual capital" that supported what Lilly was trying to accomplish with practicing clergy. He recognized that our project had a clear theoretical orientation and focused on understanding the internal dynamics of clergy groups.

His response to our work encouraged us to share our "intellectual capital" with a wider audience. In 2009, Kelli and I published *Know Your Story and Lead with It: The Power of Narrative in Clergy Leadership*[15] in order to distill, clarify, and share what we had learned in the project. In 2023 the book has continued to be used by clergy, clergy groups, and theological educators. It has been assigned reading for the Residents in the Ordained Ministry program in the North Carolina United Methodist Annual Conference.

Kelli and I owe a debt of gratitude to John Wimmer, program officer in the Religion Division at the Lilly Endowment, who criticized our second grant proposal, accurately citing where we had fallen short of our predicted goals in our first grant. However, he also became a supportive consultant, helping us to know how to apply for our second grant. With his counsel we got that grant, which made it possible for us to write the book. We were saddened to get the news that John Wimmer died on June 24, 2020. He had served as a program officer at the Endowment for almost twenty years.

THE CONTRIBUTION OF THE SOLE PERSON OF COLOR IN THE PROJECT

Our book, *Know Your Story and Lead with It*, does not include an account of the influence of race and caste on what we did together. Fortunately, as you have read above, Dorothy, an African American woman minister, participated in the project. Although she was the sole person of color in her group and in our entire project, and although at times she felt like an outsider, she did not bail out of it. In conversations with me more than nineteen years after her participation in the project, Dorothy told me about her experience there. We are fortunate to have her bear witness to her experience in the group and to give us a personal reference point to consider the alternative

---

15. Hester and Walker-Jones, *Know Your Story*.

narrative of race and caste that we couldn't see during the time of the project. I am thankful that in this book I can pay tribute to her for what she gave to the project and what she's given me in this retrospective about her.

THE KEYS

Two ideas, two fundamental themes in narrative work, informed this project and shaped what happened in it: (1) Parker Palmer's rule of no fixing, no saving, no advising, no setting each other straight, and (2) there's always another story.

There's always another story—the other story, the unacknowledged story in our project, was race. We didn't address it. We had one Black member but did not give attention to how she and the group dealt with her Blackness. Nor did we deal with the collective Whiteness of the rest of the group. We missed a real opportunity for a conversation about race, about our *diversity*. Why? The most likely reason for this oversight was colorblind racism and White fragility—both of these are *ineffable*. They were invisible to us; we could not see them.

Despite the neglect of attention to race, the project worked diligently on *belonging*. That included hospitality, working with early childhood memories, getting help with cases of pastoral leadership, and hours of mentoring by pastoral counseling center staff.

The book we published told the story, the *narrative* of the project, *Know Your Story and Lead with It: The Power of Narrative in Clergy Leadership*.

QUESTIONS

1. What educational experiences have you had in which you could tell your story to thoughtful, curious listeners who gave you their undivided attention without criticism or an attempt to change you?

2. What is colorblind racism? Was there a time when you realized you suffered from it? What helped you to see this?

3. What story can you tell about White fragility and how it has appeared to you?

4. What response do you have to the author's acknowledgments of his shortsightedness?

9

Conclusion by an Unfinished Teacher

I HAVE GONE FORWARD in this book with two fundamental convictions. First, I believe I have something distinctive to say about the practice of teaching and learning—that effective education requires an experience in which students' inner textbooks are opened and engaged. This requires teachers to be curious about and honor these inner textbooks and to speak from their own inner textbook. And within this student-teacher experience, the students relate what's in their inner textbooks to the subject matter of the course.

Second, I believe that I have been teaching in the fortress of White supremacy but have only recently been able to see this. Although this fortress has been invisible to me, it is not invisible to Black people. They have to live every day with the reality of the oppressive power of this White fortress. It affects every area of their lives.

In this manuscript, I have woven together these two convictions—what I want to contribute to the enterprise of teaching and learning, and how my Whiteness has influenced this contribution. The book, then, has become a dialogue between teaching and learning on the one hand and, on the other hand, raising to a conscious level my previously hidden assumptions about race and class.

The book brings into view Paulo Freire's understanding that good teachers possess a certain kind of security. It's not the false security of those who act as if they know it all. It is the security of teachers who know they are unfinished, who know their ignorance, and who know there is much for them yet to learn. He says that secure teachers, those who embrace the fact that they are unfinished, live with an open-ended curiosity toward life.[1] I have tried to write these chapters with such an open-ended curiosity. And I hope that in this effort I have been able to come close to Freire's concept of the good, unfinished teacher.

> Writing this book is an act of redemption
> where I reexamine and rewrite chapters
> that describe my approach to education
> and show how Whiteness has influenced
> what I've written.
>
> The rewriting has begun to change
> the way I see myself and the world.
>
> I seek to understand
> my Whiteness and its effect
> on people of color, but
> I will never be finished with this.
>
> I continue to explore how
> God does God's work of
> justice and racial reconciliation
> and do my best to join God
> in that work.
>
> In all of this I am unfinished.

---

1. Freire, *Pedagogy of Freedom*, 120–21.

Bibliography

Adler, Alfred. *What Life Should Mean to You*. New York: Dutton, 1958.
Alexander, Bobby C. "Pentecostal Possession and Grotowski's Ritual Projects as Social Protest: A Critical Assessment of Victor Turner's Theory of 'Ritual Anti-Structure' as an Interpretive Tool." PhD diss., Columbia University, New York, 1985.
———. *Victor Turner Revisited: Ritual as Social Change*. Atlanta: Scholars Press, 1991.
Allen, Jonathan. "Pulitzers Honor Darnella Frazier for Cellphone Video of George Floyd Murder." Reuters, June 11, 2021.
Alter, Robert. *The Hebrew Bible: A Translation with Commentary*. Vol. 1, *The Five Books of Moses*. 3 vols. New York: Norton, 2019.
American Legion. "American Legion Boys Nation." N.d. https://www.legion.org/get-involved/youth-programs/boys-state-boys-nation.
Andersen, Tom, ed. *The Reflecting Team: Dialogues and Dialogues About the Dialogues*. New York: Norton, 1991.
Anderson, Harlene. *Conversation, Language, and Possibilities: A Postmodern Approach to Therapy*. New York: Basic Books, 1997.
Ansbacher, Heinz L., and Rowena R. Ansbacher, eds. *Alfred Adler, Superiority and Social Interest: A Collection of Later Writings*. Evanston, IL: Northwestern University Press, 1964.
Arkin, William M. "Exclusive: Classified Documents Reveal the Number of January 6 Protestors." *Newsweek*, Dec. 23, 2021.
Baldwin, James. *The Fire Next Time*. New York: Random House, 1993.
Bonilla-Silva, Eduardo. *Racism Without Racists: Colorblind Racism and the Persistence of Racial Inequality in America*. Lanham, MD: Rowman & Littlefield, 2014.
Boswell, Benjamin. *Confronting Whiteness: A Spiritual Journey of Reflection, Conversation, and Transformation*. Nashville: Upper Room, 2022.
———. "Identifying Whiteness: Discerning Race Through Spiritual Practice in the White Dominant Church." DMin diss., St. Paul School of Theology, 2020.
Bracy, LaVon W. "I Integrated Gainesville High School in 1965: The Scars Endure." *Orlando Sentinel*, Feb. 15, 2017.
Brown, Rita Mae. *Starting from Scratch: A Different Kind of Writer's Manual*. New York: Bantam, 1988.
Brown, Robert McAfee. *Theology in a New Key: Responding to Liberation Themes*. Philadelphia: Westminster, 1978.
Coates, Ta-Nehisi. "The First White President: The Foundation of Donald Trump's Presidency Is the Negation of Barack Obama's Legacy." *Atlantic*, Oct. 2017.

Bibliography

Cobb, John. *Jesus' Abba: The God Who Has Not Failed*. Minneapolis: Fortress, 2015.

Coen, Ross. "Sundown Towns." Black Past, Aug. 24, 2020. https://www.blackpast.org/african-american-history/sundown-towns.

Condorcet, Marie Jean Antoine Nicolas de Caritat, Marquis de. *Sketch for a Historical Picture of the Progress of the Human Mind*. Translated by June Barraclough. London: Weidenfeld and Nicolson, 1955. Originally published as *Esquisse d'un tableau historique des progrès de l'esprit humain* (Paris, 1795).

Cone, James H. *The Cross and the Lynching Tree*. Maryknoll, NY: Orbis, 2011.

Crossan, John Dominic. *The Dark Interval: Towards a Theology of Story*. Sonoma, CA: Polebridge, 1988.

———. *In Parables: The Challenge of the Historical Jesus*. San Francisco: Harper & Row, 1973.

Curry, Kim. *The Sunland Training Centers: Florida's Institutes for Children with Intellectual Disabilities*: Florida Public Health Review, 2013.

D'Angelo, Bob. Review of *Blood, Sweat, and Tears*, by Derrick E. White. *Sport in American History*, Oct. 5, 2019.

DiAngelo, Robin. *White Fragility: Why It's So Hard for White People to Talk About Racism*. Boston: Beacon, 2018.

Doan, Robert E., and Alan Parry. *Story Re-Visions: Narrative Therapy in the Postmodern World*. New York: Guilford, 1994.

Dobbs v. Jackson Women's Health Org., 597 U.S. ___ (2022) (Amicus Curiae Brief of Howard).

Dodd, C. H. *Parables of the Kingdom*. 3rd ed. New York: Charles Scribner's Sons, 1961.

Foucault, Michel. *Power/Knowledge: Selected Interviews and Other Writings*. New York: Pantheon, 1980.

Freire, Paulo. *Pedagogy of Freedom: Ethics, Democracy, and Civic Courage*. Translated by Patrick Clarke. Lanham, MD: Rowman & Littlefield, 1998.

———. *Pedagogy of Hope: Reliving Pedagogy of the Oppressed*. Translated by Robert R. Barr. New York: Continuum, 1992.

———. *Pedagogy of the Oppressed*. Translated by Myra Bergman Ramos. 30th anniversary ed. New York: Continuum, 2002.

Funk, Robert W., et al. *The Parables of Jesus: Red Letter Edition, the Jesus Seminar*. The Jesus Seminar Series. Edited by James R. Butts. Sonoma, CA: Polebridge, 1988.

Gengler, Michael T. *We Can Do It: A Community Takes on the Challenge of School Desegregation*. New York: Rosetta, 2018.

Giddens, Anthony. *The Constitution of Society*. Oakland: University of California Press, 1984.

Guess, Teresa J. "The Social Construction of Whiteness: Racism by Intent, Racism by Consequence." *Critical Sociology* 32.4 (2006) 649–73.

Harris, Cheryl I. "Whiteness as Property." *Harvard Law Review* 106.8 (1993) 1707–993.

Hearn, William Patrick, ed. *The Annotated Huckleberry Finn*. New York: Norton, 2001.

Herzog, William. *Parables as Subversive Speech: Jesus as Pedagogue of the Oppressed*. Louisville, KY: Westminster/John Knox, 1994.

Hester, Richard L. "Memory, Myth, Parable, and the Therapeutic Process." *Individual Psychology* 43.4 (1987) 444–50.

Hester, Richard, and Kelli Walker-Jones. *Know Your Story and Lead with It: The Power of Narrative in Clergy Leadership*. Herndon, VA: Alban, 2009.

Bibliography

Holloway, Jonathan. "The History of Minstrel Shows and Jim Crow." Guilder Lehrman Center for the Study of Slavery, Resistance, and Abolition, July 2014.

Iati, Marisa. "Inaugural Poet Amanda Gorman Says She Was Racially Profiled by Security Guard Outside Her Apartment." *Washington Post*, Mar. 6, 2021.

Jenkins, Jennifer. "Fatal Police Shootings Are Still Going Up, and Nobody Knows Why." *Washington Post*, Feb. 21, 2023.

Jennings, Willie James. *After Whiteness: An Education in Belonging*. Theological Education Between the Times. Grand Rapids: Eerdmans, 2020.

Jones, Robert P. *White Too Long: The Legacy of White Supremacy in American Christianity*. New York: Simon & Schuster, 2020.

Kerr, Michael E., and Murray Bowen. *Family Evaluation: An Approach Based on Bowen Theory*. New York: Norton, 1988.

King, Charles. *Gods of the Upper Air: How a Circle of Renegade Anthropologists Reinvented Race, Sex, and Gender in the Twentieth Century*. New York: Doubleday, 2019.

King, Martin Luther, Jr. *I Have a Dream: Writings and Speeches that Changed the World*. Edited by James Melvin Washington. San Francisco: HarperSanFrancisco, 1992.

Knox, Olivier. "Amanda Gorman's First Political Memory Is Her Mother Reading Her Miranda Rights." *Washington Post*, Jan. 20, 2021.

Langer, Susanne K. *Philosophy in a New Key: A Study in the Symbolism of Reason, Rite, and Art*. Cambridge, MA: Harvard University Press, 1942.

Levine, Amy-Jill. *Short Stories by Jesus: The Enigmatic Parables of a Controversial Rabbi*. New York: HarperCollins, 2014.

Light, Steve. "Why 'Race Riot'? On the Need to Change a Misleading Term." *Los Angeles Review of Books*, Nov. 12, 2016.

Loewen, James W. "Goldthwaite." History and Social Justice, N.d. https://justice.tougaloo.edu/sundowntown/goldthwaite-tx/.

———. *Sundown Towns: A Hidden Dimension of American Racism*. New York: New Press, 2005.

Manaster, G. J., and R. J. Corsini. *Individual Psychology: Theory and Practice*. Chicago: F. E. Peacock, 1982.

Marshall, Kendrick. "Tulsa Race Massacre: For Years It Was Called a Riot. Not Anymore. Here's How It Changed." *Tulsa World*, May 29, 2021.

Martin, Clarice J. "Womanist Interpretations of the New Testament: The Quest for Holistic and Inclusive Translation and Interpretation." In *I Found God in Me: A Womanist Biblical Hermeneutics Reader*, edited by Mitzi J. Smith, 19–41. Eugene, OR: Cascade, 2015.

McGoldrick, Monica, et al. *Genograms: Assessment and Intervention*. 3rd ed. New York: Norton, 2008.

Miller, Alice. *The Untouched Key: Tracing Childhood Trauma in Creativity and Destructiveness*. New York: Doubleday, 1990.

Oklahoma Historical Society. "The 1921 Tulsa Race Massacre." https://www.okhistory.org/learn/tulsaracemassacre.

Oliver, Mary. *New and Selected Poems*. Vol. 1. Boston: Beacon, 1992.

Palfrey, John, and Kristen Mack. "Capitalizing Black and White: Grammatical Justice and Equity." MacArthur Foundation, Aug. 26, 2020. https://www.macfound.org/press/perspectives/capitalizing-black-and-white-grammatical-justice-and-equity.

Palmer, Parker. *A Hidden Wholeness*. San Francisco: Jossey-Bass, 2004.

Bibliography

Poetker, Katrina. "Domestic Domains in the Gospel of Mark." *Direction: A Mennonite Bretheren Forum* 24.1 (Spring 1995) 14–23.

Powers, R. L. "Myth and Memory." In *Alfred Adler: His Influence on Psychology Today*, edited by Harold H. Mosak, 271–90. Park Ridge, NJ: Noyes, 1973.

Scott, Bernard Brandon. *Hear Then the Parable: A Commentary on the Parables of Jesus.* Minneapolis: Fortress, 1989.

Sloane, Martin E. *The Diminishing Barrier: A Report on School Desegregation in Nine Counties.* Washington, DC: U.S. Government Printing Office, 1972.

Spain, Rufus. *At Ease in Zion: A Social History of Southern Baptists 1865–1900.* Nashville: Vanderbilt University Press, 1967.

Swirko, Cindy. "Alachua County Confronts Its Racist Past." *Gainesville Sun*, Feb. 28, 2020.

Turner, Victor. *Dramas, Fields, and Metaphors: Symbolic Action in Human Society.* Symbol, Myth, and Ritual Series. Ithaca, NY: Cornell University Press, 1974.

Tutu, Desmond. *God Has a Dream: A Vision of Hope for Our Times.* New York: Doubleday, 2004.

Twain, Mark. *Adventures of Huckleberry Finn.* London: Chatto & Windus, 1884.

Walsh, Kenneth T. "50 Years After Race Riots, Issues Remain the Same." *U.S. News and World Report*, July 12, 2017.

White, Derrick E. *Blood, Sweat, and Tears: Jake Gaither, Florida A&M, and the History of Black College Football.* Chapel Hill: University of North Carolina Press, 2019.

White, Michael, and David Epston. *Narrative Means to Therapeutic Ends.* New York: Norton, 1990.

Wilkerson, Isabel. *Caste: The Origins of Our Discontents.* New York: Random House, 2020.

Wink, Walter. *The Powers That Be: Theology for a New Millennium.* New York: Doubleday, 1998.

X, Malcolm. *Autobiography of Malcolm X.* New York: Grove, 1966.

Yacovone, Donald. "How Textbooks Taught White Supremacy." *Harvard Gazette*, Sept. 4, 2020.

———. *Teaching White Supremacy: America's Democratic Ordeal and the Forging of Our National Identity.* New York: Pantheon, 2022.

———. "Teaching White Supremacy: U.S. History Textbooks and the Influence of Historians." Charles Hamilton Houston Institute for Race and Justice, Mar. 6, 2018.

www.ingramcontent.com/pod-product-compliance
Lightning Source LLC
Chambersburg PA
CBHW031432150426
43191CB00006B/486